Civilians at War

Civilians at War

JOURNALS 1938–1946

George Beardmore

JOHN MURRAY

© Victoria Knowles and Anthea Meadows 1984

First published 1984
by John Murray (Publishers) Ltd
50 Albemarle Street, London W1X 4BD

Typeset by Inforum Ltd, Portsmouth
Printed and bound in Great Britain
by The Pitman Press, Bath

British Library Cataloguing in Publication Data
Beardmore, George
Civilians at war.
1. World War, 1939–1945—England—London
2. Harrow (London, England)—Social life and
customs   3. London (England)—Social life
and customs—20th century
I. Title
942.1'86   DA685.H2/
ISBN 0-7195-4161-1

Contents

Illustrations

ACKNOWLEDGEMENT

Nos 8, 9, 10, 11 and 13 by courtesy of the BBC Hulton Picture Library

Foreword

George Beardmore was born in 1908 in the Potteries, in Staffordshire. His father's family were 'small farmers on the Derbyshire borders but about 1780 they took to industry',* as ironfounders. The second son of a well-to-do ironmonger in Burslem, his father Frank served his apprenticeship as a potter and then, anticipating his inheritance, bought a partnership in a firm which eventually bore his name, in Fenton. Frank married Sissie Bennett, eldest daughter of Enoch and Sarah-Ann Bennett. Sissie's brother Sep was employed by Frank Beardmore 'in the design of vases featuring peacocks, tall ladies in flowing draperies, and gloomy cypresses . . . what became known in the trade as "Old Greek".' Her eldest brother was the writer Arnold Bennett.

Enoch's influence was to have a devastating effect on his children and indeed upon generations of the family. He had 'by murderous endeavour' taught himself to be a solicitor at the age of 34. 'The most painful characteristic of every member of the Bennett family, except for the children's mother, was the absence of any sort of sentiment. Tenderness had been rooted out, crushed, and burnt in the interest of intellect. None of them knew what love was or, if they did, they were at pains to hide it . . . "Sustained effort" and "Duty" were the first words impressed upon them.' George himself knowingly inherited this puritan background from

---

* All passages in quotation marks are from an unpublished autobiographical memoir by George Beardmore or from the introductory chapter by him to *Arnold Bennett in Love*, 1972, the correspondence between Bennett and his French wife, Marguérite Soulié.

his mother and struggled against it all his life. He compensated later by marrying a gentle, witty and graceful girl. Speaking of his mother he was to say: 'After her death in 1939 we children listed sixteen public offices our Mother had held, starting as a certified midwife and going on to become a Red Cross quartermaster, president of the local British Women's Temperance Association, District Food Officer during World War One, chairman of this and that committee and capping all by being made one of the nation's first women magistrates.'

In 1913 Frank Beardmore went bankrupt and had the furniture of his home bought for £500 by Arnold Bennett, who then handed it back into Sissie's care. It was for this reason that George and his brother were sent to the local Council school, rather than educated privately. George progressed to the Middle School at Newcastle-under-Lyme, 'a provincial boy with the broadest of accents and narrowest of outlooks'. His father 'failed but undefeated', was working in London as a potter's agent, his mother as North Staffordshire Organiser for the Coalition Liberals, 'a lost cause but at least one for which she was paid'.

George's first job was a five-year stint in the offices of an insurance company in Hanley. In 1931 he and his family moved to North Harrow, and he transferred to the City office of the firm. In the same year his first novel, *Dodd The Potter*, was published. A succession of unsatisfactory jobs and unpublished novels followed. He married his wife Jean in 1935 and his father died in 1936. His second novel – 'pure story with everything in it, rape, white slaves, and murder', called *The House in Spitalfields* – came out in 1937. In September 1938 he was 30 years old and he and his wife were living in a house in North Harrow. 'Our avenue of semi-detacheds and almond trees curved up from Headstone Lane and at its top end, where we lived, had the Kodak factory playing fields on one side and on the other a willow wood. When the bombing started, because of the absence of shelter from other buildings, we became particularly vulnerable to blast.' He was commuting every day to a job in Regent Street in the West End where he was under notice to quit.

Preface

These journals came to light when moving house in 1977, that is, over thirty years after they had been compiled. They were written on scrap paper, discontinued office circulars, and the like, and they were bound in twice-used folders whose clips had rusted to become immovable, evidence of the scarcity of paper in those days.

An attempt was first made to remove the more personal notes and present the journals simply as an account of people met, rumours heard, opinions held, and incidents witnessed in the changing scenes and fortunes of war. It then occurred to me that mine had been pretty average circumstances and were representative in themselves of a large body of the middle-class without claim to celebrity. War is a great disturber and, as in almost every other household, jobs came to be changed, a home given up, babies born, and parents widowed. So my fortunes, too, now appear to have been a reflection of the times and have not been omitted. The journals are reproduced largely as they were written although some changes have been made, a great deal of outdated family gossip has been left out, and material added from recollection (in brackets) if only because the entries were often made under stress.

Where I was not average lay in the fact that I was a writer – had indeed two novels to my credit – with an instinct to note down what I saw and heard. Could I overlook, in the interests of fiction, that this was the first time in over eight hundred years that the people of England, particularly of southern England, had found themselves in the front line and under bombardment? Of course I couldn't. So as opportunity presented itself, I made notes.

GEORGE BEARDMORE, Dorset, 1979

1938

About time I started a Journal again as events crowd upon us. Today we spent 25/- on sugar, rice, flour, corned beef, and Marmite which we have stored in the sideboard against the day when these things will be difficult or even impossible to obtain by reason of War. This morning the Prime Minister returned from his Godesburg conversations with Hitler and although the outcome has yet to be discussed in the Cabinet before being made public, I am far from unique in thus preparing for the worst. The issue is that if Herr Hitler marches into Czecho Slovakia to aid his so-called subjects, France declares war on him, we join France, Russia joins us, and together we overwhelm Germany. That's the theory. My chief concern follows a recollection of the 1917 bread queues, but for myself, I can't worry about events over which I have no control.

After a brief talk with Corky (the family doctor), it appears that Jean has filled a true bill and may safely be called a prospective mother. At last! The event should take place about 20 May next.

I should be happier if I knew that I had a job to go to after 31 October next, which is my last day in Regent Street. Four prospects present themselves: the BBC, Odham's, sale of a book, and the possibility of my successor proving a failure.

27 September

We were all waiting for Hitler's speech at the Berlin Sports Palace last night to show some conciliatory spirit but instead it demanded evacuation of the Sudeten region, intact, by 1 October. Otherwise he threatened to march. Today therefore has seen Jean collecting our gas-masks, and loud-speaker vans patrolling the London streets recommending Westminster residents to be fitted with masks, but after working-hours as Whitehall was already packed with some 14,000 applicants. Harrow is placarded with red bills asking for nurses and ordering John Citizen to call at the nearest school for his mask. Outside Westminster City Hall this lunch-hour I saw eight big cleaning vans being loaded with big square tins, presumably holding masks. One always assumes that Whitehall knows best but all its efforts seem to be devoted to making and distributing gas-masks. Poison-gas? But surely it was proved to be a two-edged sword in 1917 by blowing back into the Huns' faces. Perhaps here-after we shall have our south-west gales to bless as well as the Channel.

Also saw a load of sand outside a Pall Mall club and sandbags lining the walls of another. Holland says that Clapham Common is being dug into trenches by the light of flares. Five central Underground stations are to close down, those centering on Charing Cross. This is said to be so that fire-proof and flood-proof doors can be installed. The Thames isn't far off, after all. Yet apart from the tension inside oneself and the inevitable turn of conversation London runs along as usual, the streams of traffic, the old lady selling chrysanths on an Oxford Circus corner, the foun-tains blowing in Trafalgar Square.

Jean has made up her mind to go to Horsham (i.e. Love's Farm, where we spent part of our honeymoon) but only if the threat is carried out so drastically that life cannot be borne. After all, she says, Harrow is fifteen miles from Marble Arch. I didn't care to remind her that a plane would do it in under five minutes. Her face is very sad and I play patience with her and make tea, much as I dislike both these diversions in the evening. As Corky tells her, she is now responsible for another life.

My next-door neighbour, Amos, has agreed with me to begin work tomorrow on an air-raid trench in his garden to take eight sitting, with an adit at right-angles: his idea. He's more farsighted than me. He says: 'No need to make it a home because we shan't need to be in it more than half an hour at a time', which is the opposite of what the official bills, posters etc. tell us.

Tonight the PM has given a long and moving broadcast. He sounded tired to death and despondent, but with a wonderful naturalness touched with anger when he spoke of the 'fantastic' notion of our going to war for a people (the Sudetens) of whom we know nothing, and bitterness when he mentioned Hitler's unreasonableness. The sincerity of his inflection moved me very much.

At this moment it's pouring – I hear the gutters bubbling houses away – so work on the trench tomorrow seems improbable.

28 September

The day broke fine and I was at work by 8.30 a.m., clearing the ground, and only gave up at 11.30 a.m., three feet down, when a heavy drizzle set in. Now Amos has dug to five feet and I shall take time off tomorrow to try to dig deeper. Funny thing, even at five feet one finds bindweed roots.

The Staff was paid today as the firm expects the joint-stock Banks to declare a moratorium. I drew out £15 and as my monthly credit has not been passed through I am now overdrawn by £6-odd. Overdrafts don't seem so important these days. Increased tension in the City, we are told. Frank Taylor (Jean's uncle) and her mother set out for Buckinghamshire this morning to try to find a hideout for herself and her sisters but came back without having had any luck. What cottages there had been vacant had long since been taken. Luckily the Loves have wired that Jean and I can have the Shack at the farm, but only after we had suffered much anxiety. I wonder whether to join Air Raid Precautions. My nightmare is of being conscripted and separated from Jean, while her brother Jack has the same fear of being separated from his Mary.

Parliament met to hear the Premier's report. The meeting was drawing to a close when Lord Halifax handed him a note. It was Hitler's assent to a joint meeting of himself, Chamberlain, Daladier of France, and Mussolini of Italy at Munich. A great personal triumph for Chamberlain. Also universal relief although there has been no slacking-off of ARP activities, recruiting, and propaganda. The BBC still gives the news in three languages.

29 September

Only an hour's work on the trench today although Amos has put in two. As a PT instructor and Games Master at Harrow County School he has more muscle than I have.

People are still flocking into the country. The LCC's evacuation of its 500,000 schoolchildren to unknown destinations has taken place. The Assistant Secretary's view is: 'This would bloody-well happen over our annual audit.' One meets now and then people like him who can look at the crisis level-headed and refuse to be stampeded. From a purely personal point of view, I had hoped that if the crisis and recruiting went on much longer some job would be bound to fall vacant. But it turns out that the crisis has thrown yet more men out of work. In hopes, I put an ad in yesterday's *Telegraph* offering my services.

30 September

No, the LCC did not evacuate its 500,000 children but they were on the point of going, and detailed instructions had been given over the radio as to the clothes, food, and money they were to take with them, and the kind of billets they might expect to find at the other end, when at 12.15 this morning the Four Power meeting came to an agreement. The PM has stayed on today for further talks with the Fuehrer. A joint statement was issued this afternoon stating that war was never again to be resorted to and that differences would be settled by consultation.

Nevertheless ARP is to continue – are to continue – and we are to retain our gas-masks. Funnily enough, the Assistant Secretary became anxious on hearing the news. He said: 'That settles it. I'm off home to take the wife and kid to Aylesbury, and blow the annual audit.' Dollar back at $4.75 to the £.

No change in my own affairs. Having nothing to do I walked round the British Museum this afternoon and was again more struck by the excellence of the housing of the exhibits than by the exhibits themselves. I say 'again' because the V & A struck me like that, except that the iron jewellery fabricated by the Parisians, to replace the gems they had handed over to pay for munitions during the 1870 siege, was topical. Somehow I don't see my wife handing over her engagement-ring whatever the extremity. Poor dusty Westminster Abbey is so cluttered with rubbish that it has lost its sanctity. During the past week Intercession has been in constant progress round the Unknown Warrior's tomb.

1 October

My Saturday off. Wrote 3½ pp. of Chapter Eight of *The Undefeated*, equal to a thousand words. Coughing a lot during the day. October was always a sticky month for asthmatics.

Politically a revolution of feeling has set in. The First Lord, Duff Cooper, has resigned because he distrusts the foreign policy that has just brought peace to Europe but by the sacrifice of Czecho Slovakia. Others will follow, Anthony Eden for example. Winston Churchill as one might expect is not in favour of what has come to be called 'appeasement'. We ought to have made a firmer stand, they say, otherwise that fellow across the North Sea will tear off country after country like leaves off a calendar.

4 October

Visited the Unemployment Board where I filled up a detailed form that included a request for the names of the Principals of my schools. How crazy can you get! Pinkerton in Glasgow (I learned) is no more, although old Flogger Wood is still walking the streets of Stoke-on-Trent at 85 years of age. A most depressing place. Situations Vacant pasted up and scanned listlessly by two or three youths in mufflers. A sharp-tongued civil servant behind the counter made it clear that you were unemployed and he wasn't. An ante-room like a public lavatory with a notice saying Smoking Not Permissable (sic) hanging askew on the nail, brown and curly with age. The same kind of smile on the face of each boy as he was called up to fill in his form. From start to finish, the process was made humiliating.

Also visited the office of the Clerical Workers' Union in Snow Hill which I had joined when in difficulties with H. in Bishopsgate. The same middle-aged gentleman in a small cluttered room. He reminded me of Conrad's Mr Verloc who 'had an air of having wallowed, fully dressed, all day on an unmade bed'. He offered me a cup of tea but no suggestions as to how to find a job. He said: 'They come in here all day like you. What can I do?'

6 October

On the off-chance I visited the City after a long absence and found that by far the pleasantest part of the excursion was coming away from those tall depressing palaces and grey-faced men. Father once commented on the unsmiling intent faces of City men. All the same, the City has proportions and grandeur in its buildings not to be found in the West End which, comparatively, is dirty and tawdry.

Called in at Lombard Street (in which stood my first London office), shook hands with my old pals, and came out with mixed feelings. True, their jobs were secure, but there they still were, treading the same mill and growing sleazier and more disillusioned. I didn't envy them one bit. To be frank, I felt more experienced than any of them, as though recently returned from the Congo and hopeful of soon going up the Amazon.

10 October

Jean sleeps a great deal and apart from being a little sick every morning is well, as usual. Funny thing, we haven't talked or prepared much for the baby. Not only my future is in doubt but all Europe's, with that fellow goose-stepping about holding torchlight processions.

29 October

Yesterday I was invited by Maurice, first lieutenant to the great C.B. Cochran, to look him up at the Grill Room, in the Trocadero. Found him rehearsing his 'kids' and the sumptuous Grill Room in the hands of charladies, carpenters, and odd-job-men; a new act in progress, straight from the US via the Holborn Empire and the Alhambra, two acrobatic comedians. Swart, formidable little men very concerned about a tour of Europe, including Germany, that they had been booked for. Maurice took me round the back and showed me the 'kids' ' dressing-room – a little cloth over each tray of cosmetics, shoes in a rack over the mirrors, baubles over the shoes, and all the dresses stacked in order of appearance behind a runway valance. Asked him what would happen if war broke out and he said: 'Pouf! Everything and everybody would go into the ragbag, including me.'

1 November

Following tradition, on being fired I treated the office (sixty-seven of them) to a cake apiece for tea. They in turn had raised £3 towards an electric clock which I fitted into position this morning. The present was not sponsored by the Executive. Officially I have been fired because, although efficient, I 'don't bring in new business'. Well, Dad always said that I couldn't sell bread to a starving army. The real reason for my dismissal is not quite so obvious. Although my thriller had come out under a pseudonym, the ad for it in the *Evening Standard* had carried a photo of me. Even so, I thought I would be pretty safe because the likeness wasn't a good one, but when I came back from lunch one day, remarking on how unnaturally preoccupied the typists appeared, I found my desk swept clear and the damned advertisement drawing-pinned to it. As a burst of girlish laughter rang out I told myself: 'George, I give you three more months in this place.' Actually, it turned out to be two.

Dreaded going to the Labour Exchange after my experience with the Unemployment Board and walked all round Wealdstone trying not to find it. Surprised therefore to find the clerks very pleasant. I was officially signed on and given a card and told to come with my 'books' in two days time.

4 November

Nice genial place, the Labour Exchange, even though it smells a bit and the language is a bit raw. No suspicion here of officiousness. The men chaff the clerks and the clerks have their own private jokes. One or two angry-looking youths with pamphlets in their pockets, 'Soviet' this and 'Workers of the World' that. A burly man under 'Vacancies' asked me about myself and told me to drop in on him once a fortnight. 'Kodak', he said mysteriously, 'are bound to expand.' Youths called on him and he would call out, 'Sorry, no carpenters', 'No fitters'. Very well organised – your card gives you the two days of the week when you are to call, and the time. So it's 'nine o'clocks only, please', and 'nine-fifteens the other side.' You are also told the counter you are to attend. The clerks tear off calendar numbers for counter numbers as these apparently change from day to day. They use a kind of 'dub', or smooth-worn handle, to poke the many cards in and out under the bronze grille between them and the queues. Innumerable cards and leaflets to fill up, including one for Jean, to show that she doesn't work or keep lodgers. The net result – 27/6d a week, plus another five bob when the baby arrives.

11 November

Total eclipse of the moon on the night of the 8th, not that it made the least bit of difference to anyone.

The farcical feature of politics is its hypocrisy, the theory apparently being to bluff the other chap. Hitler says: 'We are a peace-loving nation', and in the next sentence talks of the present glorious state in which Germany finds itself, with every able-bodied man conscripted. Even Neville Chamberlain at the Guildhall Banquet tried to reconcile 'we are go-getters for peace', with the fearsome increase in armaments.

Myself, I have made up my mind that I am a-political. The only strong feelings I have are directed against those who try to impose their will on others, whether it's a father getting his belt to his son or one country telling another: 'Do this, or else'. But even that is emotional, arising from the matriarchy under which I was brought up. Jean finds it incredible that I was once subject to fits of hysteria.

(Later) Following the assassination of a German diplomat

in Paris, said to be by a Jew, the most appalling general pogrom broke out at 2 a.m. this morning all over Germany. Jewish shops in Berlin were looted and set on fire while the police looked on. Jews were forced to jump from second-storey windows, and to crawl on their knees for a mile or two. An old man was beaten along the street while a 13-year-old girl tried to protect him, screaming at the mob. The news is that Jews have been lynched, forced to resign their property, and sent to concentration-camps. It's a new St Bartholemew's Day Massacre.

An old lady, the mother of a friend of Jean's, was in Berlin during the recent crisis. She knew nothing whatever about it. Her relations phoned and wired her to return but she just wondered what all the fuss was about. Only when she went to the British Embassy did she get any suspicion that Germany was on the point of going to war with her country. She was not allowed to bring any money out of Germany and gave it all to friends, leaving herself with only five Marks which she gave up at the frontier. She reports that the ordinary German housewife doesn't know what white bread is. If she (the housewife) buys one pound of white flour she has to buy four pounds of black at the same time, willy nilly. She never sees onions for sale, and very rarely fresh fruit. Church-going is proscribed. To go to church worshippers leave their home secretly at eleven at night, go up the avenue, down a street, cross a field, and enter a farmhouse where a room has been consecrated. Or such was this friend's experience.

What was I saying about the imposition of one will on another?

At 11 o'clock on this day last year, when recovering from scarlet fever, I watched the House Surgeon come out of the Diphtheria Ward and stand bareheaded in the rain. Some bitter personal memory of the 1914/18 dust-up, I daresay.

17 November

World-wide indignation at the massacre of the Jews in Germany. A fine on the community of £80 million, no Jew to hold any sort of office or to carry on trade or to go into a theatre or cinema. All the damage done to Jewish shops recently to be put in order by the Jews themselves before they hand their shops over to Aryans.

General terms such as 'Jews' don't mean much to me. When I hear the word I think of Adolf Kohn and his wife from whom I used to collect two guineas a week rent for three rooms on the first floor of a Fournier Street, Spital-fields, tenement. The first person I saw on mounting the stairs was little Becky out on the landing finishing off shirts. Inside the workroom, which wasn't more than sixteen feet square, was Adolf in his shirtsleeves working a steam press, Mrs Kohn running up shirts, a baby slung in a sort of hammock, and sometimes an old, bearded, partly blind man seated in a straight-backed chair reading a book printed in braille. Overhead was a tangle of wiring – their constant complaint, when it wasn't the behaviour of the Pakistanis sharing a yard with them, was blown fuses. The last time I called on her, hearing that I was going to be replaced, she gave me a salmon rissole and a cup of tea.

I shouldn't like to think of the Kohns being ill-treated because of a cover-all word like 'Jew'. The big question is whether or not I would be prepared to fight for them. How I hate hypothetical questions. Almost as much as being dictated to.

7 December

Luck may have turned my way. Had a letter and subse-quent appointment at Mortlake. The firm is a sweat-shop notorious in the insurance profession, long hours and lots of worry with the prospect of being turned out as soon as your job is done. Saw an underling, as I guess, and was short-listed and told to wait for an interview.

Finished *The Undefeated*, largely a story about my father and the Potteries. I think it's all right but that's not to say it will sell.

22 *December*

Visited Mortlake again. Bitterly cold. Snow and ice had been shovelled into packs round Mortlake Square. I must have walked round it four times before going in to face the interview. Eight other fellows were lined up on a bench outside an office door marked 'Director', and a ninth came out looking sheepish, smiled at us, shook his head, and took his seat alongside the rest of us. Inside the office was a tall man with a long face, Jewish extraction I should imagine, leaning against the shelf over the gas-fire. The man I had spoken to at the first interview did the talking. He was seated behind a desk. I thought, 'Well, here's another job down the sink, now I can start another book', when the tall man interrupted, saying that my being dissatisfied with £5 a week at my last job and the fact that I wouldn't start at less than £4 here showed me to be the wrong type. This made me so wild that I lost patience and asked him how I was expected to stay honest at £4 a week in a firm with a turnover of thousands. He asked me to go outside and wait with the others on the bench. Ten minutes later the tall man stuck his head out and asked: 'Which is the one whose wife is having a baby and won't take less than £4 a week?' I followed him inside where he said: 'The job's yours. Start on 2 January. Would you like an advance to see you over Christmas?'

Sounds like a story-book but that's how it was. The effect on Jean was immediate. She had soldiered through the last three months but had obviously been distressed. Now she said: 'It's late but I can still make the cake.'

Twelve degrees of frost. The pipes froze but I thawed

them out with hot-water bottles, lying flat on my belly in the filth of the loft.

More snow. Drifts everywhere, grass not to be seen, birds frozen on the bough, snowballing, delayed posts and trains. All our presents are posted and all our forty cards. Mother's friend, Mrs Moody, has left us a prodigal supply of grocer's delicacies. So all's well.

30 December

The old year of invasions and threats of war hasn't finished with us yet. Cycled to Watford in the slush and fog to pawn Dad's gold pencil and the ring Jean gave me and only got thirty bob for them. An odd recollection came back of the first office I went to, under protest, at Hanley, Staffs. At age 18, with five subjects passed in the Higher School Certificate, I was given £40 a year. On the windows, by way of advertisement, were printed the words: '£217,000,000 in Reserve', the shadow of which fell across our backs as we bent over our desks. I don't suppose the oldest of us was getting more than £110 a year. Hitler or no Hitler, that's why wars are fought.

1939

---

18 March
Hitler marched into Bohemia on the 14th, entered Slovakia a day later, and now stands armed giving ultimatums on the Rumanian border. In this and similar circumstances a chap like myself, only too happy to be left alone, begins to notice indignation rising within himself. This must mean that the rest of the country is noticing the same indignation in themselves, perhaps more so. Here, I tell myself, is the point where a tyrant must be stopped.

2 April
Boat-race day at Mortlake yesterday. A mass of aeroplanes passed overhead just as Cambridge was winning by three lengths.

10 April
A pleasant leisurely holiday very much assisted by day-long sunshine. Good Friday started with Mussolini's invasion of Albania. The threat of a major war is so much with us that we have got into the way of ignoring it. The Cabinet met today. Chamberlain, poor devil, had to cut short his fishing in Scotland, and even Roosevelt was impelled to return to the White House. But the general public took its holiday unperturbed. We saw some 200,000 of them at Regent's Park Zoo this afternoon. To return to Friday, while Jean dozed on the lawn I cut the grass for the first time, weeded paths, and hoed. In the evening we suddenly got out of our armchairs and went up to town where we had dinner at the

Coventry Street Corner House. Everything anybody does now is 'for the last time, before it comes'.

28 April

The nation has so far reversed its nine-hundred-year-old policy of isolation as to 'guarantee' unlikely places like Greece and Poland. President Roosevelt also has written a personal letter to the Fuehrer and the Italian Duce asking them for a promise not to appropriate any one of thirty named countries. Nearer home, conscription was put into operation this week, beginning with men under twenty. The Bill comes before Parliament next week, while a first-class recruiting campaign is in full swing both for the Territorials and for National Service. Well, here I am, a married man of 30 with a son only a month away and a full-time job. If conscripted I'll go willingly enough because that would be unavoidable and outside my control.

The firm has decided to give Staff contracts in 'approved' cases. Three of the senior men are not 'approved' and in fact McG. is on the brink of being given his cards, E. is already fired, and H. is under notice. Notwithstanding this the Secretary had previously told us all that we were not to get panicky, that our jobs were safe, etc. etc. As McG. said to H.: 'Acting like Hitler has become fashionable.' This is because the latter's promises (we had a large dose today, relayed to the world from the Reichstag) and solemn vows have so often been belied by his actions, which have included the grabbing ('liberation') of Austria, Czecho Slovakia, and Memel, all in the last six months.

29 May, Whit Monday

According to tradition, an expectant father tramps up and down the parlour until he hears a thin wail upstairs. I should still be waiting for the wail. Jean woke me on Saturday night at 3 a.m. not knowing whether some uneasiness she felt was wind or the first tugs. The pains have been growing worse ever since but she is still walking about. We slept at her mother's last night, at the top of the road, or rather, I did for I don't believe that Jean got a wink. She is still there, lying down in her slip trying to forget things.

All this follows a twelve-hour stint at the office on Saturday.

30 May

Have just left her at the nursing-home, pupils wide with the sedative Corky gave her. She slept well for two hours and is still a trifle silly. The sudden tearing spasms, that leave her suddenly and unaffected, are like nothing else I've ever witnessed. If I wanted to be facetious I should exclaim with John Halifax, Gentleman: 'Ere that almond-tree blooms again I shall be a father.' Well, perhaps J.H.G. didn't have a fifty-minute rail journey to his office, eight hours when he got there, and another fifty-minute rail journey back home.

Incidentally, nothing to do with the impending baby, I am inspecting motor-bikes in hope of buying one so as to cut the fifty minutes journey to the office down to thirty.

4 June

Mamma (Jean's mother) came knocking on the front door at 5.30 on the morning of the 31st to announce that a daughter had been born an hour before. Jean was well, she said. Curiously enough, three neighbours saw or heard Mamma knocking at the door, even at that hour, and guessed the reason. The only thing they didn't deduce was the baby's sex. When I saw her, Jean was fast asleep and in so thorough a way, in such a posture, with such an absence of colour, that I was torn to the roots by the suspicion that she'd gone. However, in the evening she looked bright as ever and very sorry for not having been awake to greet me. In the morning the baby looked a bit blue about the cranium but normally red in the evening. A new life, by God, whatever 'life' is. Jean is now feeding her with a look on her face I have never seen before.

Decided to buy a small Royal Enfield (£8) if only because, if war is to come, it will be essential to have mobility, I mean apart from trains which might be brought to a halt or requisitioned or whatever.

Mild criticism has been levelled at me for sleeping on the night the baby was born, and less mild criticism for going back to bed after Mamma had brought the news. I don't know what Jean's parents expected me to do all night, except behave like John Halifax, Gentleman. There's something else, too, implicit, that one can't explain to people. I *was* with her while she was having the baby just as she was with me while I was tramping round Mortlake Square in the snow and ice before going in for the interview for the job. Neither words nor presence are necessary.

21 *August*

Mother died this morning. When I last saw her, at Coton Hill, her memory had gone but she was able to say when I told her that Jean was soon to have a baby: 'How happy it will make you.' I had wondered how I was going to be able to pay the nursing-home fees, buy a pram and so on, but happiness had never crossed my mind. So she could still surprise.

The Secretary asked me to keep an eye on M. while the post was being opened this morning. This ceremony takes place in the basement where the mail-bags are emptied onto a trestle-table and six or eight clerks stand round sorting out the letters. Money arrives in all shapes: cheques, postal-orders, loose notes, sometimes loose change. I saw M. stuff a miscellaneous handful into his trouser-pocket and instantly realised why the Managing Director had been so struck by my use of the word 'honest' at our interview. The

Secretary charged him and the wretched M. held out two notes as though they had been red hot. He confessed to numerous thefts, and three postal-orders came out of his pockets plus a couple more notes. He was taken to Mortlake Station and charged again, and released to appear before the Bench on Friday. The whole business depressing beyond words.

A tremendous downpour-cum-thunderstorm this afternoon. One flash almost paralysed Jean who at the time was nursing the baby, having just come downstairs to take in the telegram about Mother's death. I rode my motor-bike through submerged streets and my shoes became filled with water.

War is obviously on its way. Some days are like that.

28 August

This is written at Love's Farm, near Horsham, on a perfect summer evening. This afternoon I went bathing in Horsham park and burnt my back on the hot concrete. Jean had taken Victoria, the newest member of the family, for a walk to Brooks Green and met one parson and two cyclists on the way. Not a sound except for clucking hens, a motor-cyclist changing gear two miles away, and a goods-train rumbling twice as distant.

Not a hint anywhere that a European war is only hours away! The wireless has just given out that Holland has mobilised, our navy has taken over merchant shipping, Sir Neville Henderson is flying back to Berlin with the Cabinet's answer to Hitler's latest proposals, London schoolchildren are already labelled ready to be shifted out to the country in trains already assembled, London is ringed with bombers (or so the optimistic rumour goes) ready to take off and lay Berlin in ruins – and I don't doubt that Berlin has its bombers, too.

Mother used to relate how to the last Father had sworn

1 George and Jean Beardmore at the time of their engagement in 1935

2 and 3 Jean and George hatted, in the 1930s

4 George's Mother, Frances, sister of Arnold Bennett the writer, in 1935. '. . . the matriarchy under which I was brought up.'

5 George and Jean with Victoria, 1940

that the First World War would never break out, and I daresay he used the same words as me: 'Fellow wouldn't be so mad.' Hitler has brought Germany back from chaos to become one of the foremost states in Europe. Now then, would he chuck everything away on the risk of the outcome of war? He must know that he wouldn't be allowed an easy retirement to Doorn, like the ex-Kaiser. On the other hand, is he one of the long tradition of tyrants who must always go adventuring if he is to stay in power? The latest is that he has alienated Japan by making that extraordinary, out-of-character pact with Russia. In spite of the present alarming symptoms – the *Europa*'s failure to call at Southampton, the cessation of international railway and air traffic, the Emergency Decrees as to billeting, black-out, and the Bank rate – I am still optimistic.

Last week was the grimmest I've had to suffer since Dad died. Attended the magistrates' court at Mortlake but wasn't called to testify against M. because he pleaded guilty. He was discharged under the First Offender's Act provided he joined the army.

Early on Wednesday afternoon I set off for Stoke on the motor-bike. Near 40 m.p.h. the machine begins to shake with what my father-in-law calls cyclic periodicity so I was some hours making the 150-mile journey. Found the family unchanged, quarrelling like the kings at the court of Agamemnon before they set off for Troy, with my sister Margaret playing the part of Clytemnestra. Cremation next day at Stockport, Cheshire.

A long time ago, while still at Penkhull Infants School, I had trotted off to Stoke Station with a pal of mine called Jenk. He said that 'something was up' there and, sure enough, we found the forecourt packed round the statue of Wedgwood with army ambulances, horse-drawn drays covered with straw, cabs, carriages, motor-cars – every kind of four-wheeled conveyance. On the other side of the lines,

where the London trains came in, a long long train stood
disgorging passengers. And when we had run hallooing
through the echoing subway we found the gates shut against
a whispering crowd of women and old people peering
through at a platform filled with khaki-clad men, many on
stretchers, all wearing bandages and square labels, and
most of them filthy and muddied as though they had just
stepped out of the trenches. Among them were nurses, one
of them my mother. There she stood, bonnet strings flying,
disguised by her scarlet and blue cloak and starched white
dress with the red cross on it, flinging out her arm in a
typical gesture as much as to say: 'Well, pick him up, pick
him up, don't just stand there.' Such was my recollection as
we knelt in the gloomy chapel.

Margaret had a splendid meal waiting for us but I left
before the sweet, mounted the bike, and came home. I
couldn't make it quickly enough but had to put up with the
same bone-shaking 38 m.p.h. all the way down the A5. A
convoy of army lorries outside Lichfield but otherwise no
overt signs of war. And here I am conveniently on holiday,
waiting for a war to be declared or for yet another 'Munich'.

1 September

Jean had been sleeping away from me all week so that the
baby should not wake the Loves in the next room, but this
morning she joined me after she had fed the baby, and we
were glad and have been all day, for the comfort and
communion it afforded us. We needed all the comfort we
could get for in the 10.30 a.m. wireless news we learned
that Germany had invaded Poland and that therefore, because this country had 'guaranteed' Poland, both France
and Britain had mobilised.

Big personal shocks at first leave me unmoved and their
force only makes itself felt after half an hour. So it was
today. Jean wept a little. The whole scene is mixed up for

us with a row in which Mamma became involved with Mrs Love, chiefly on my account. Mamma swore that she would sooner be bombed at home if she had to be bombed at all. The result was that I was given urgent instructions to find transport back to London for the three of them – Jean and her mother and the baby. My father-in-law is already at home: as Maintenance Engineer at Broadcasting House he has been working a fourteen-hour day and sometimes sleeping on the premises. As for me, I had the motor-bike.

Here I am at home in Harrow, therefore, waiting for the taxi to arrive with Jean and the baby in it. The whole of England is in total darkness, weird to experience, and I am more afraid for them now than ever I was while the baby was on its way into the world. The Guv'nor (my father-in-law) has been down here helping to pin blackout paper over the kitchen and nursery windows. A watch-committee is patrolling the neighbourhood on the lookout for exposed lights. I saw Mrs Rendell defying them from her front doorstep as she would defy the Archangel Gabriel. One of the strangest sights encountered on the way home was a London double-decker bus speeding along between Guildford and Woking with a cargo of schoolchildren. The vast and elaborate plan for evacuating children, and for all I know the sick, aged, and crippled, from the country's industrial centres must be in progress. But the National Gallery, I wonder, the treasures of the British Museum, the Science Museum, the great libraries – what is being done to save them? I want to be everywhere at once to witness and report.

3 September

Was interrupted writing the above by the Guv'nor. We sat up until 1 a.m. waiting for the taxi. He's in a dead funk most of the time which leaves me feeling guilty because I am not: anything outside my control doesn't seem to worry me. Went to bed intending to lie awake but slept. The family did not arrive until 6 a.m. on Saturday, yesterday. The taxi had been travelling only on sidelights. Poor Jinnie! Poor baby! The latter had had her morning feed in the taxi, God knows how. Some world she's been born into! The avenue at night seems hostile in its silence. Harrow by day on the other hand is crowded and feverish. A terrific thunderstorm last night went unremarked. I applied for a job as a Special but was told that the waiting-list had been full for months. So I shall put in to be a Medical Orderly, and should I be called up, join the RAMC if I can. Something constructive at least.

(Later) Jean up and cheerful as ever. We might have known that in the blackout, with nothing to distinguish between Putney and Vauxhall, and driving only on sidelights, the taxi-driver would lose his way. The four of them spent the early hours wandering round south London. Makes you wonder how many more families got lost last night, trying to reach their homes.

(Later) It would be impossible to convey the sense of utter panic with which we heard the first Air Raid warning, ten minutes after the outbreak of war. We had all taken *The Shape of Things to Come* too much to heart, also the dire prophecies of scientists, journalists, and even politicians of the devastation and disease that would follow the first air raid. We pictured St Paul's in ruins and a hole in the ground where the Houses of Parliament had stood. But nothing happened.

4 September

For the first time we saw the police in steel helmets. The Specials had also been called out and the roads are thick with police. Lads after the stamp of the Head Filing Boy ('boy' by courtesy – he's over 50) stand in khaki and steel helmets on duty at Richmond Bridge and along the railway

lines. Yellow notices have appeared in railway carriages
telling passengers to lie on the floor in an air-raid, having
drawn the blinds to stop flying glass. (George Edgar, one-
time soldier of the First World War, said you'd not catch
him lying down on the floor of a railway carriage.)
Announcement after announcement over the wireless relating to billeting, closing of schools, evacuation, addresses
of public concerns like the licensing offices, where to
apply for gas-masks etc. Special dispensations to Catholics,
notices that sports meetings are to be abandoned, a plea
from the RSPCA – one goes to the wireless to be thoroughly
disheartened.

5 September

There are supposed to be 8,000 barrage balloons up. They
hang over London like ephemeral coconuts, bunches of
them, pearly and softly gleaming, nosing their way through
the magnificent clouds we have been having lately.

We had the second air-raid warning at 3 a.m. but I went
to sleep in the middle of it, as did Jean, and like the first it
turned out to be just another unidentified aircraft although
this time somewhere over the Midlands. They are building
a gun emplacement in Richmond Park and rumour (from
one of the chaps at the office) reports that Pen Ponds, in
Richmond Park, are to be drained to prevent the arrival of
sea-planes. (Isn't that going a bit far? They can't drain the
Thames.) Notices have appeared at street corners pointing
out Air Raid Shelters. I am taking classes in First Aid
organised by the firm. Also the filing-boys are digging up
the garage floor with the idea of providing our own Shelter.
Of course, such conditions, of not knowing what's happening, are fertile ground for rumours. The latest is that the
Germans have filled hundreds of toy balloons with poison
gas and released them over the streets of Warsaw to be
picked up by children.

6 September

The first true air-raid, carried out (we are told) over the Ford motor-works at Dagenham. No damage done but a customer from Hornchurch saw a plane brought down in flames. It occurred at 7 a.m. and was over two hours later but the effect, just when people were going to work, was to create the longest traffic queue in history. We had been told that in the event of an Alarm sounding, all vehicles must come to a standstill and space left for ambulances and fire-engines to get through. Milkmen must have had special instructions because I saw one lead his horse into a side-road and tie its head to a tree. It's this sort of thing that makes one believe the people in Whitehall never learned a thing from the Spanish Civil War and are just guessing – issuing edicts under the Defence Regulations because they look good on paper. The Alert caught me on my 250 c.c. Royal Enfield at the top of Hanger Hill and I was another two hours making it to Mortlake, travelling in first and second. I could have fried an egg on the cylinder-head and the clutch is down to the metal.

There is a feeling of wrath that since war has been declared, why haven't we wreaked our worst on Berlin. All we have done – and this we *have* been told – is rain down on north Germany some tons of leaflets. Cartoonists depict Hitler on his knees begging us to rain famine, bombs, and gas on Germany but not the truth. Perhaps this is to be the new mode of warfare – persuasion. Perhaps both sides are too much afraid of the weapons they have at their disposal.

7 September

C.B. Cochran's secretary paid me a visit and told me that after his first holiday in five years he had been thrown out of work. Now, starting Monday next, he is to earn £4 a week driving a Lyons van. All the theatre staff is out and not so lucky. Likewise the television stations. The cinemas throughout the country are closed although what are described as 'non-evacuable areas' (my God, this jargon!) can have their cinemas open on Mondays provided they shut at 10. Unemployment, in short, is today an even greater threat than Hitler. As for the office, our staff of seventy is virtually idle. We play cards and read newspapers from 10.30 a.m. The rationing of petrol (I am to receive 2 gallons a month!) has given the firm its last kick. This being my late night I was able to get in a long talk with the Director. He told me that tomorrow thirty-five of us are to be given our cards – but I am not one of them. He even suggested that if the firm closed down entirely I might make a good caretaker. But he rubbed in that if I could get another job I should do so, and the Secretary later confirmed that it was a case of every man for himself. In my innocence I had thought it was that anyway.

Apart from unemployment the general feeling is that we are engaged in a picnic. But then we are reminded that in August 1914 the war was thought to be a picnic but the imperishable retreat from Mons followed and with it the bitter winter of that year. Also, we cannot regard the 1914 war as a precedent. Now we are out to down a régime, not a nation. Now we know the full disaster of war and, more than this, we all know that we *must* fight or be dominated by a gang of bullies and liars. It's the lying that I can't stand, any more than the Secret Police, the Concentration Camps, the rubber bludgeons, the plucking of Rabbis' beards, burning of synagogues, the lack of honour.

South Africa has come to our help and declared war, and predictably America has declared her neutrality. Well, as to the latter, I wonder what '*Lusitania*' will bring them in at a later date.

The sides and running-boards of cars are to be whitened. In the dark, picked out by sidelights, they look like skeleton-cars.

8 September

Went on my bike to fetch a radio from Welwyn Garden City for the Director. General impressions are of soldiers on the move, low-flying aircraft, and fear of unemployment. However, the radio factory is in full swing, I was told.

10 September

This is one of the most mysterious wars through which I have ever lived. Mysterious because nobody knows what's happening. A paucity of news over the radio. Is anything happening? No cheering crowds, no drafts leaving Victoria, no indication indeed that we are to send an army abroad. But then, if we are leaving poor battered Poland with the idea that we can somehow slide out of a major offensive, it's time we threw out the Peace Premier Chamberlain (71) and got someone more belligerent in his place.

17 September

Have just nipped down to listen to the 6 p.m. news and learn that Russia invaded Poland this morning on the pretext that Poland no longer existed as Poland and that she (Russia) had to look after her interests there, i.e. the part of the Ukraine in Poland. I cannot remember having prophesied before that this war is going to involve every European country, America and Japan as well, but I shall be fairly safe in saying so now. Lithuania is on the brink, Roumania too. The question is, who's going to come in on our side? All those who should are studiously cultivating neutrality. Warsaw has not yet fallen.

At 9.10 p.m. we are able to listen to Nazi propaganda emanating from Hamburg. A priggish voice, betraying the German only in the long words. One wonders who the speaker is. The truth sounds very different coming from Germany. One might almost think, listening to him, that it is we who are being fed a pack of lies. Some of the perversions of fact are a bit crude, considered as an art in fine lying.

Some of our own press contains all the silly rancour that one reads curiously in the Lambeth Imperial War Museum as having been published for truth between 1914 and 1918. The 'Hitler – Wanted for Murder' series, for example. *War Illustrated* could have served a good purpose but has chosen to flare its headlines with raw adjectives that only irritate.

I myself have had a bit of luck, or is it? The BBC is expanding and the Guv'nor has found a job for me at Broadcasting House. Only as Assistant Storekeeper, it's true, but at five bob more than I am getting here, and secure, at least until the war ends. After the Mortlake firm, it's like being taken under the wing of a big old Rhode Island Red. Still, a very different occupation from that originally envisaged at Broadcasting House. Perhaps, who knows, once in it I can get a transfer. Jean badly wants me to take it for security's sake, and at least I shall be in the centre of things. At Mortlake, three of my pals have been given notice and only seventeen remain. Start tomorrow – no notice required, in the circs.

28 September

Almost another fortnight of war has gone by, and we are still very much in the dark as to what is actually going on. At this moment Ribbentrop (German Foreign Minister) is seeing Comrade Stalin and the result is feared to be a constructive alliance on the foundation of the unexpected non-aggression pact. Yesterday Sir Samuel Hoare brought in the first War Budget ('Boodgit' as Snowden used to call it) and pronounced the phenomenal figure of 7/6d in the pound income tax, with reductions, thank heaven, for wife and children. Also unexpected increases in the price of tobacco and beer – 1d on the pint. Lord Camrose, owner of the *Telegraph*, has been introduced into the Ministry of Information, which was reported in the Commons to employ a staff of 999. Let's hope he brings a bit of style to it. At the moment it dishes out information the public already knows in the dullest possible way. Of course, the public is longing to hear about sensational exploits by air, sea, and land, of batteries wiped out and woods occupied and air squadrons engaged over enemy lines, our gallant airmen emerging infinitely superior. What we get is one sentence to the effect that a German sortie has been repelled with loss, that the Saarbrucken salient has undergone nightlong bombardment, and that enemy aircraft were seen over the Dutch border. Churchill, bless him, gave a splendid account of the navy the day before yesterday – so much contraband seized in excess of tonnage sunk, so many submarines disposed of and so many merchantmen preserved. One or two fine literary asides about the reliance to be placed on hostile accounts of fabulous engagements in which our capital ships are sunk. He is very popular indeed, notwithstanding that on the 18th the aircraft carrier *Courageous* was sunk by torpedo with the loss of just over half the crew of 1100-odd.

No more raids recently. One learns (from Ivan M. who should know) that the first raid was absolutely genuine, that on the outbreak of war at 11 a.m. on Sunday the 3rd a German squadron rose to bomb Portsmouth, that one and a half minutes later English planes were up to intercept them and drove them back. The second raid was a frost, and in fact an English plane was shot down by our own AA. The third was also genuine, with losses on both sides somewhere over north Kent and the estuary.

We still wonder whether our masks and gas-proof rooms will ever be necessary. An ARP Warden knocked at 11.30 p.m. to complain that the landing window showed a reflection from the 'glim' in the nursery. We say the Wardens' zeal will cool with the frosts and rains of the war's first winter.

My third book, *The Undefeated*, has sold. It's a sign of the times that, in order to get into print, I had to sell it outright. All the same, it means Jean can have new stockings and that the half-yearly rates can now be paid. I still take sandwiches for my lunch but this week I treated myself to hot lunches at the Poly in Regent Street, a gross extravagance.

7 October

Have never yet been in a job where I had to do so little and yet get praised for it. Why, to stay until 6.30 p.m. last Thursday was considered a hardship. 6.30 p.m. was the usual thing at Mortlake until recently. Why then am I bored to tears and miss the cheer of Mortlake fellowship?

Hitler (no longer accorded a 'Herr' either by statesmen or announcers, so why should I) made claim to the old German colonies yesterday. Given them, he would be willing to make peace with France and ourselves. Or so he said. None of us can be proud of our record as the proprietors of colonies – at the school debating society I put forward the proposition that colonies were the fruits of wholesale robbery, and was heavily defeated by the history master's son – but the Germans have the worst record of any of us, not excepting the Portuguese, for oppression and extortion. At least we went far towards uniting India by providing a common language, roads, and railways. It's historical fact that the Germans, in Africa at least, were only interested in loot.

The Hamburg English announcer has described the first of the war-songs – 'We'll hang out our washing on the Siegfried line' – as being in bad taste.

At the pictures on Tuesday we saw a newsreel of the troops in France. They seemed very old-fashioned, and one expected the film to grey over with speckles and flicker, like the old newsreels. Coming home in the pitch dark was an experience. All the streets were deserted as though plague had struck and the death-cart had made its daily collection. No children at play, no lovers up against lamp-posts, no sound, and only an occasional chink of light under a front door or the glow of a cigarette. It all seems very humiliating, this cowering down in expectation of death falling from the heavens. In fact, the plague-years must have been very like this.

15 October

The BBC has now made up its mind that all Temporaries are to go, so I leave on Saturday next. The job was so utterly boring and lifeless that I am glad to be forced to look elsewhere. As the 23-year-olds have now been called up I shouldn't be long out of work.

The *Royal Oak* was sunk yesterday. The posters were reading 'British Hold Part of the Line' when I walked up Foubert's Place for a coffee at 11.15 a.m. When I came back they were reading '*Royal Oak* Sunk'. The loss of hands is the most terrible part, only 400 saved out of 1100. Otherwise the German Government is going round appealing for peace – to Italy, and to the USA – and being snubbed.

22 October

Yesterday was my first day of unemployment this year. Handed in my cards at the Milton Road Exchange, waiting two hours because of the crush, and got signed up. Tuesdays and Thursdays at 11.30 a.m., Box 8. Room crowded and more outside, but only about three other 'jacket-men', the rest artisans and labourers. Yesterday was also the signing-up day for all the 20/21 class but I didn't see any of them and suppose they had been told to report elsewhere.

Sovereigns, if any, are now worth 39/6d. Hamley's of

Regent Street have their latest toy in the main window – 'Build Your Own Maginot Line'. On show is a cross-section of the tiered dug-outs and little men in them doing a variety of duties, a blimp hung up from a lorry outside, and an advance patrol crawling through the heavily camouflaged country, meeting with heavy fire. All right, it's only a toy, but a sudden realisation was brought home to me that, historically, purely defence-positions have never held out for long. Or hasn't the French General Staff read Plutarch?

Torches and gas-mask cases are for sale in Oxford Street. Here also a system of sand-bags and baffle-walls has been built round fire-alarms and police boxes. Rationing is to come in next month and even now the Government has put a top price on commodities like bacon, eggs, tea, and sugar. The BBC (when I left it) was in a state of panic following the recent German raids on Scotland. All inside-corridors have gas-proof doors at ten-yard intervals, and the front entrance is entirely bricked up except for a narrow passage through which one squeezes, pass in hand, into the gloomiest foyer ever imagined. The receptionists, well-groomed rather officious young ladies known as 'the canaries', have all gone, although their counter remains, dusty and scattered with out-of-date reading-matter and someone's forgotten cap. The BBC's Emergency Headquarters has been established at Wood Norton in Worcestershire where six hundred bicycles at £6 each have been bought for the use of staff.

An assistant at Milletts, from whom I bought a service-able gas-mask container like a coffee-tin (the ones you are given soon fall to bits), told me that almost all the staff from his and other London branches had left their respective premises at 10 p.m. last night to report to a warehouse near Waterloo Station where they spent the night assembling gas-masks. They had given up at 5 a.m., gone home to snatch what sleep they could, and come back to serve in the shop at 10 a.m. 'Double time', the assistant said. 'All good money but I couldn't do *that* every day.'

Text for the day on the tear-off calendar: 'Integrity is praised, and starves.' Words by Juvenal addressed to the dole-queues of the twentieth century.

These last two days have been truly autumnal, slight frost in the morning, bright sun all day, wet earth, and a blue mist descending about five-thirty, a smell in the air of bonfires and chrysanthemums.

27 October

Prices are slowly going up. The twopenny bars of chocolate are to be smaller and restricted to standard lines, i.e. milk, plain, and with or without nuts. Gone are multitudinous varieties such as the egg-flips, almond, grapefruit, and sandwiches. Sausages are now 7d a pound – beef, that is. The makers say that skins now cost them more. 1d is charged for delivering papers. Bread is up ½d a quartern. Lyle's Golden Syrup unobtainable, presumably because it stores well. Bacon about 1/8d. Papers must be ordered as 'returns' will no longer be accepted by the publishers. We have yet to reach the 'Sacrifice Sundays' of the Berliners but we are quickly getting to that stage.

2 November

Have been working for Wembley Boro' Council this last week, trying to find out where some of their missing rate-payers have disappeared to. Rates still have to be paid, war or no war. Mostly they have gone, I find, to relations in Yorkshire and Lancashire, and to hideouts made ready months ago. Surely out of the seven jobs I have so far undertaken (this is the eighth) this is the only one that has allowed me to come home in the afternoon for a nap – and please myself whether or not I venture out again! I put in a moderate number of calls on Monday and Tuesday, that is, arriving back home about four in the afternoon, but was tipped off by the other 'follow-upper' that I was doing too much and queering the pitch. So I laid off. The technique is simple. You have to get in touch with the missing household's milkman, who apparently knows everything about everyone, including the infidelities, and if he doesn't know, try the postman. Road-sweepers and dustmen, too, are surprisingly knowledgeable.

The number of well-to-do people who have just upped and gone is astonishing. At one house I found a back door open, walked inside, and a *Marie-Celeste* situation presented itself: breakfast-things unwashed, a half-smoked cigarette dipped in tea to put it out, fruit going mouldy in a bowl, and a mysterious note on the gas-stove that read: 'Grandma Highgate Ponds 5.30'. Made me laugh. A neighbour told me over the fence: 'You from the Council? I thought so. They've gone to somewhere in Bedford.' But another house I tried had so obviously been broken into that I dialled 999. The police-car when it arrived contained a fellow I had known briefly at the Mortlake firm.

16 November

Came home for good at 11.30 a.m. having done nothing more important than have coffee with a fellow-collector. But what a worthwhile cup of coffee that was for he told me that the gas-meter men know even more than milkmen, particularly as to where the missing families can be found. 'They have to be told', was the explanation. So I have cleverly arranged to meet the gas-meter man every Saturday morning in the local Express Dairy when he will obligingly fill in the blanks on the list given to me by the Council's Treasurer's Department. My fellow-collector also said that if I did well – and to my surprise the Rates Department thinks I am doing well – I might graduate to become rent-collector and after that, who knows, to bailiff. Now there's ambition for you. On the other hand, the Guv'nor brought news that the BBC was going to invite me to join their Installation Department on a more permanent basis.

On a newsreel yesterday Winston Churchill was loudly clapped when even the appearance of the King had been received in silence. A very youthful-looking Duke of Windsor was given an even greater hand. Now there's a fellow who fell down on his job. His present Majesty is a good conscientious man but Edward VIII in the present emergency would have been inspiring. Apparently my views on the D. of W. aren't always shared because I heard of a friend of mine who places a tumbler of water between himself and his glass of wine. This is so that when the loyal toast is proposed he can describe himself as drinking to the king 'over the water', a nice bit of casuistry that first came in with Bonny Prince Charles, after Culloden.

10 December

The last weeks have been spent at Broadcasting House employed as dog'sbody to an engineering section which, given an allotment of £100,000, builds a transmitter with it, from the aerial, masts, and condensers down to the last button. I might have been bored to tears but am much too curious about this band of highly efficient, dedicated professionals. I shan't often have the luck to be on the inside of a mystery – a business, that is, about which nothing is known – with a view to a story in the distant future. They have a half-amused half contemptuous 'Oh, God!' attitude towards the people who subsequently make use of the transmitters, regarding them as amateurs. Hadn't realised before that broadcasting is an apple with two distinct halves.

The shops are brighter and richer than ever, now the Christmas season has begun. Beats me where people get the money from to buy all the goodies. I give Jean five bob a week more housekeeping because bread, meat, milk, wood,

6 'The Guv'nor'. Jean's Father,
  Leslie Wolfenden, house engineer
  at BBC Broadcasting House

7 Jean's Mother, Helen, July 1939.
  She died aged 53, in 1943, an
  'invisible' casualty of the war

8 Madame Tussaud's Cinema. See entry for 10 September 1940

9 'The worst sight of all was the wrecked and gutted John Lewis's building in Holles Street, off Oxford Street.' See entry for 24 September 1940

pants, gripe-water have all gone up their 2d or 4d or 6d. Also next year's rates are bound to go up with the expenditure on ARP, building of public shelters etc.

Jean not at all well, having lost 7 oz in 7 days. Care of the baby plus worry about the war. How many others like her, I wonder.

31 December
All ages from 20 to 28 are to be called up, in stages. And so to 1940.

1940

These mornings I catch the train at Headstone Lane, change to the Underground at Finchley Road, get off at Baker Street and walk, seeing what I can on the way. Nothing unusual to report these days but perhaps, following a tradition started in classical days or before, the war will become more urgent in the spring. I have a room to myself on the fourth floor, opposite Features and Drama. Ironical, really – there am I writing up orders concerned with millimicrofarads when across the passage the creative stuff is going forward. Or am I well out of it? Meanwhile I contrive to write about 500 words a day of the spy-thriller under a cover of a scribbling pad. I write semi-shorthand in very tiny script halfway through the pad so that when anyone puts his head round the door I seem to be adding up figures. Also I am protected from discovery by the improbability of finding a cost-clerk writing a novel under his scrap-pad.

The war is uneventful and marked more by surprises like butter-rationing and the rise in the cost of living than by the firing of guns. The milk bill now comes to something like 7/- a week, the coal (1 cwt of anthracite costs 3/4d and 1 cwt of coal 3/1½d) to over 6/-, meat we cannot buy except in scraps. Eggs are plentiful and cheap. We are rationed to a quarter of a pound of butter each and with great altruism I have margarine so that Jean can have plenty, with a bit over to give to her mother. Petrol is 1/10d a gallon. Rumours of 'pool' (i.e. mass-made) suits to come and a prodigious rise in the price of woollens.

20 January

This last fortnight has brought a cold that has almost frightened me. One night no amount of hot-water bottles would warm my bones and by day I walked round feeling like an exposed skeleton. We are not badly frozen compared with others, who have flooded kitchens and damp walls.

28 January

Extreme cold. The railway carriages are full of talk about bursts, ice in the bath, and flooded carpets. The intense cold makes me queasy but, thank God, no return of the asthma. For the first time I saw snow in Oxford Street, not just a scattering but banks and lanes of it, worn down to ice in places and in others piled as high as one's head.

At least the war machines are kept immobile.

19 April

A week ago Germany invaded Denmark and Norway. Not much hard news otherwise available. Such was Jean's fear when she first heard of it that she phoned me at the office to be sure to bring home my gas-mask. And so I did – once. Chiefly I think she wanted to be reassured. Not long ago she said, out of the blue: 'Georgie, it's going to be all right, isn't it?' to which I replied: 'If we stick together.' Perhaps I ought to have replied: 'If we are allowed to stick together.' Very few gas-masks are carried these days, the theory being: 'Even if they come, they won't drop gas, not the first time.' Women (meaning Jean) are so much more realistic than men.

How we look forward to the Churchill broadcasts! Everyone adores him, if only because he warned us of the German threat years ago. He contrives to endow the word 'Nazi' with supreme contempt, and his literary phrases, such as when he spoke of the Dutch being 'penned in the same cage as the tiger', put new life into the news. 'We have had no naval successes in the North Sea,' he says, 'because we have not been able to find any enemy ships.' As well as the dramatic content of his speeches there is often an item of brand-new information. That's what we are starved of – information.

The 27 age group is to register within three weeks. Then a further Royal Proclamation must authorise enlistment of those (say) up to 41. I am thought to be in a reserved occupation.

Strange that the neighbourhood at home is being visited by billeting officers, seeking out rooms for Civil Servants from the north. For one thing I should have thought that the said Civil Servants would do well to stay where they are, and for another, not long ago the Civil Servants in Harrow were being evacuated in a hurry to the north.

21 April

That word 'invasion' comes glibly off the pen but what does it mean apart from the business of war? What will it mean to Denmark for instance? The arrival of those packed troop-carriers, one imagines, tanks, and a staff car with a strutting officer getting out of it. Proclamations in two languages posted up. Martial law. Curfew. The closing-down of dress-shops because they are mostly owned by Jews, and the disappearance of the Jews themselves to unknown destinations. Schools given the task of teaching German – and possibily provided with a new type of history-book. Loud-speakers. Town Councils given their orders. Men who collaborate and others who don't. Neighbour looking sideways at neighbour to question the side he's on. Betrayals. Public executions perhaps – certainly public trials. A much much poorer life-style in which the right foods cannot be obtained because they have been shipped off to Germany. Husbands taken from their families and lost, perhaps forever. More than anything the humiliation that is carried round with one, even when asleep, like Christian's burden in *Pilgrim's Progress*.

Well, someday I may have to make a choice.

5 *May*

BBC staff is clamouring for a cost-of-living increase in pay. Railway fares are up 10%, clothing to go up 15% in the autumn, food up about 20%. Another 1d or 2d on anything you care to mention – either that, or the article is reduced in size, like chocolate. Woolworths are selling their sixpenny pots of paint for 8½d and threepenny shampoos for 4d. Soup is 3½d per bowl instead of 3d. Of course, even though some of these rises in prices are legitimate, others are not: the vicious practice of raising prices on stuff shopkeepers have had in stock for months is explained by the bland, 'Cost of living these days, you know'.

Last Thursday the PM announced our evacuation of south Norway. We have in fact been heavily beaten – routed. All that people like me can understand is that Germany has collected every country she has wanted. The US, as last time, is keeping out of it, but then so is the USSR.

12 *May*

Such a day as Friday last, the 10th, which began with an invasion and ended with a change of Premier, will not be seen again this lifetime. In a way people are relieved that at last the lies and pretences are done with. Belgium, Holland, and Luxembourg have, almost overnight, suffered the onslaught of the German 'blitzkrieg', after the Polish pattern, i.e. bombing and strafing by planes followed by tanks followed by infantry in overwhelming weight. (Liddell Hart was quoting a Frenchman, Charles de Gaulle, who long ago foretold that for the forseeable future this is how wars would be fought, rather than by the 1914–18 method of

taking up fixed positions and making charges and counter-
charges. Well, perhaps we shall be spared the slaughter of
another generation – and Stoke Station full of wounded.)
Everyone is asking where the Maginot Line ends and all
are utterly stupefied to discover that it doesn't extend as far
as the coast. Another three days and those armies will be
staring at us across the Channel. Of course, this invasion of
harmless countries has been denied as a possibility *thirteen*
times by one Nazi high-up or another.

All day long we have a feeling that while one goes to the
office or listens to the blackbirds – this is after all spring-
time, the only pretty ringtime – somewhere all hell is let
loose. But news of it doesn't reach us for at least a week.
Meanwhile we hear conflicting reports that German parachute troops, sent forward to capture or destroy key bridges
and strong-points, are or are not successful. One hears of
how the Allied troops – 'not a man on foot' which presumably means that they ride troop-carriers – poured hour after
hour over the Belgian frontier. Germany is said to have lost
200 planes in two days. Reports appear of Rotterdam aero-
drome captured and recaptured, of Amsterdam streets in
flames, of 200 French civilians dead in widespread raids.
But not a raid over England! Too busy elsewhere, one
supposes. The hard fact is that we know only that the Low
Countries have been invaded by the Germans. All else is
conjecture.

Chamberlain has been replaced by soldier-statesman-
historian Winston Churchill. I have always been a Churchill-
ian because he writes well, which in the circumstances doesn't
seem an adequate reason. A man of 45, Anthony Eden, has
been appointed Minister for War, and a Coalition Government formed that includes Attlee, Arthur Greenwood and
Sinclair. Everyone rejoices. The impression was gathering
that Chamberlain's government was an assembly of austere,
upright, strict maiden aunts.

Tomorrow, Whit Monday, has been cancelled as a holiday, presumably to allow the railways to function normally and to allow the nation as a whole uninterrupted labour.

15 May

Nowadays, at home, we switch on to hear the 8 a.m. news and by so doing learned this morning that the Dutch army had capitulated. The Germans are in possession of Amsterdam (a perfect take-off base for bombing England) and Rotterdam, but for some reason the approaches to Antwerp are held. At this moment, we are told, the first pitched battle of the war is in progress before Brussels. How memory irresistibly goes back to the VIth Form and Jackson saying: '– the cross-roads of Europe. Any country at war in Europe, for whatever purpose, must hold Brussels.' The Germans throw every bit of metal into the initial blow, a method that has so far succeeded throughout central Europe, in Austria, Czecho Slovakia, Poland, Denmark, and Norway. Incredible that one should be living in such times. I find myself shaking my head to bring back reality. Dreadful, unthinkable visions enter my head of what *would* happen if they won and crossed the Channel. Mentally I have already sent Jean and Victoria to Canada, and seen Harrow bombed, and parachutists seize Broadcasting House. The imagination makes these fantastic notions so real, but of course they are purely mischievous. To counter them, we heard the new War Minister last night appeal for Local Defence Volunteers to deal with parachutists. That at least is something I can do. Also we are told that Germany cannot afford to spend 5,000 or whatever gallons of petrol on only one Junkers 88 to bomb England. One remembers the armies of France, the Dominions, the vigour and resolution of Churchill.

London streets are full. One sees almost as many young men as in peacetime. *Gone With the Wind* and *Pinocchio* are attracting full houses and getting all the criticisms, but plays are being replaced by revues. In my Department they are planning, estimating for, and building a series of new transmitters to be dotted over the country inconspicuously so that, in the event of invasion, some will always be in service.

News from America makes everyone angry: of all things, the President has sent Hitler an official protest at the latest invasions. Also the Americans look like dividing on the question of what kind of President to have next year, one clever enough to foresee that our war is their war, or one to pursue that old ghost, 'isolationism'. Persistent anti-Ally demonstrations in Italy are taken by the *Telegraph* to mean that Mussolini is trying to whip up his people into a sufficient hatred of us to induce them to side with Hitler.

Following a succession of hot days we had a short, terrific thunderstorm last night. The culminating peal shook the house. A red descending glow in the south-west is believed to have been a barrage-balloon, struck over Parliament Hill Fields. The portents are coming after the event.

Was in the Drawing Office just now (5.15 p.m.) when a tea-girl came up with the news that the Belgian Army had capitulated and moreover that parachutists were dropping gas-bombs through the ventilators of the Maginot Line. However, members of the Lines Section, who have just heard the 5 o'clock news, say that it's all rumour, that the French are throwing back massed tank attacks, and that in fact the parachutists have captured only one outer fortress, Liège, in the manner described. Rumour also alleges that Italy has joined in. Not a word from any source about the British sector, casualties, lines held etc.

Written in my shirt-sleeves by an open window overlooking Langham Street.

16 May

Until today I had never imagined the fear of the British between 1914 and 1918 that they *might be beaten*. (I was 6 years old when that war broke out and not likely to take serious interest in outside events.) Since then I have always known the outcome and regarded it as inevitable. The present state of affairs has made me realise that what is now in my mind was at that time in my father's. Horrible conjectures appear. It is a fact that should Britain lose, it will not be in the accepted, historical manner in which nations lose – in which, for example, the Dutch (no blame to them) laid down their arms. The typists swear that they would sooner shoot themselves than agree to any form of capitulation. I myself know as a fact that the country would be laid waste before we gave in – I mean that I am sure of it as I am sure that I sit here.

Yesterday's rumours were typical of those brought up to the Drawing Office. The Germans are held – or so we are assured. One imagines the weight of armour they are now amassing somewhere in Belgium before rushing forward in one grand overwhelming onslaught.

A true report this time (as distinct from all the rumours and placebos administered by wireless and newspapers) from Haynes of Wiring whose brother spent six unforgettable days on the abortive expedition to Andaalsness, mid-Norway. It was taken in by a cruiser and brought back under heavy shelling in a destroyer to Scapa. The Green Howards are said to have gone out with 400 men and 13 officers and returned with 90 and 1, respectively. The German bombers were 'like a bus-service', arriving every twelve minutes between 8 a.m. and 7 p.m. A raid could be expected because the RAF used to come down and retire into hiding in the hills five minutes beforehand. (The suggestion was made in the office that either the RAF didn't have enough petrol or ammunition, or that they had been ordered at all costs to their pride to save their planes for more urgent business in England.) Either way, the Navy's Air Arm felt so bitter about it that they pinched the RAF's petrol so as to send up three Skuas as a token resistance.

Some practical tips on being bombed: bombs kill only those hit directly or by shrapnel: men at Andaalsness had lain on their stomachs only ten feet from an exploding bomb and, while they may have been lifted off the ground and deafened, they had walked away otherwise unscathed. The episode was described as 'half-hearted' and 'a farce from the start'. The conjecture was that it had been undertaken only as a gesture.

We are now waiting for Italy officially to join with Hitler. The impression one gets is that nobody much fears the Italians, after fighting with them in the last war. Essentially they are not a warlike nation. 'A better enemy than ally' is one description. Still, one wonders how they would have been described had they been on our side.

22 *May*

Last night at about 9.10 p.m. one had the impression of all England bent over its wireless-sets as we learned that German advance troops had taken Arras and Amiens, names familiar from the previous war, only a short distance from Abbeville and the coast. Reynaud, the French Premier, gave out the news in the afternoon, alleging that the enemy's speed was due to a failure to blow up the Meuse bridges. One waits for a counter-attack which Duff Cooper promised last night would be 'formidable'. One imagines that when the objective of the coast towns is attained, the troop-carrying bombers will be diverted to landing in this country, laying Canterbury waste and its cathedral a crumbling grey ruin such as Rheims cathedral was left twenty-five years ago, besieging places like Manchester, turning our own selves into refugees trudging down

English roads and lanes that have suddenly become hostile. All these horrors are possibilities at this moment. Although the rumour is that my department will be evacuated to Droitwich, Jean has decided to stay at home, although she might take the baby to Freda's (my sister-in-law's) near Wetherby in Yorkshire. Even so, Droitwich and Wetherby are only fifteen minutes or so away by bomber.

No hard news about the British Expeditionary Force. How many of our men does it muster, and where are they now?

The general mood I should say is one of growing anger. I felt it last night when I went to Kenton to collect a cot for Victoria, who is now standing up. By then Reynaud's news had sunk in. First there was Marsh, now in the Ministry of Supply and while there an Air Raid Warden. He said that twenty-three years ago almost to the day he had been one of those who had cleared Arras of the Germans. I saw tears in the eyes of this homely fellow, living three doors away, when he said he recalled the friends he had lost there. Hetty, whose cot I was borrowing for the next three years, said that she and her 4-year-old Christine were staying in their home, come what may. Her husband, Alfred, came home about 8 p.m. He is employed by Stoke Newington Boro' Council in Food Supply. They are taking in a Belgian refugee, a woman of thirty. On the way home I was helped by a tall, sturdy, and very grubby young man who said he was due soon to be called up and was meanwhile making all he bloody well could (as an electrician) by dint of working twelve hours a day and at week-ends so that he would have something to leave with his wife. His work took him inside the barricaded Admiralty. Finally George Edgar said that the situation was as bloody as it could be, speaking as an old soldier, and he had switched the wireless off and was taking his missis to the pub, even with beer at 11d the pint.

The worry was enough to wake me at 4.30 a.m. As

torrents of rain had fallen, breaking a three-week drought, I couldn't use the Enfield to get to work and took a Workman's ticket at 1/0½d instead of 2/8d and arrived at Baker Street at 8 a.m.

A Bible outside a church in Baker Street was open at the passage: 'I will lift up mine eyes unto the hills from whence cometh my help.' Very apt, I daresay, but the psalmist didn't specify which hills and whether he had a German blitzkrieg followed by invasion in mind. Still, it comforted because it took one's mind back to invasions long ago.

I forgot to say that should the Alert go at night we have decided that while Jean picks up the baby and her mattress I should (1) fill the bath, (2) empty the pantry of its mops and mangle and black it out by means of the moveable shutter I have fabricated, (3) get the wireless going, and (4) run a lamp and lead from the hall light to the pantry. Somehow, I don't see all this happening, not at once anyway. We consider the pantry safest because it is under the stairs which will shed descending rubble and because its window has very little glass, and is shielded by next door.

28 May

I imagine that for the last three days all this country and France has been waiting for some masterly and overwhelming counter-attack. Gamelin has been sacked and perhaps shot, and Weygand put in charge with the 84-year-old Petain, whom I remember from 1918, to advise him. Foch and Haig alas are dead. (At the Council School we were given little sticker-stamps with pictures on them of all the generals, admirals, etc. Some of them have since been execrated as mass-murderers, but not Haig or Foch.) But presumably we are still in retreat – not that we have much firm land left to retreat to. This morning at 8.30 a.m. Reynaud told the Chamber of Deputies that the Belgian Army had surrendered under instructions from King

Leopold and against the advice of his ministers. However, a later rumour has it that the army is disobeying Leopold and fighting on. If true, the official news of the surrender would be catastrophic for in that case the BEF would be left out on a limb. At 10 a.m. the paper-shop had sold out but I got these details from the man behind the counter (this is the kiosk at Oxford Circus) after hearing rumours from old Charlie Hunt at Broadcasting House. But already the lift-man knew, the roadmenders, and the women at their street doors.

I ought to explain that, having moved from Broadcasting House to Langham Street, the department has now moved to Bentinck House in Bolsover Street, which is rather a sleazy neighbourhood. I still have a room to myself but whereas I formerly overlooked two lovely auburn-haired girls finishing, ironing, and packing dresses, I now watch Mr H. Lynch, Boot Repairer, at his last. He puts a number of tacks in his mouth and neatly spits them out one at a time. All the same, odd to find a cobbler's, a tob. & con., and a greengrocer's so near Oxford Circus.

As a collector of rumours I have heard that (1) Germany has requested a 24-hour armistice in which to bury the dead in front of the Maginot Line (2) Lord Haw-Haw – since identified as William Joyce, an Irishman – has promised from Hamburg that when the bombings begin Harrow School (because Churchill went there) and HM Stationery Office (where the leaflets of the early raids were printed, also situated in Harrow) will be among the first targets (3) an old newspaper-woman living at Bushey noticed a blind man reading a paper which led to the discovery that a local blind school was a nest of spies. 'More tomorrow', as the comics say.

By the way, 'Haw-Haw' isn't a good or accurate nick-name. A peer who speaks condescendingly through his nose might be called 'Haw-haw'. Joyce has a heavy voice like that of an old-fashioned schoolmaster, loaded with sarcasm. However, I guess the name is here to stay. His brother was employed by the BBC until he was found in the News Room without good reason, when he departed.

The broad-beans are flowering profusely but somehow one can't spare time to consider broad beans and their perfume these days. I have been comforted by the reflection that *when* we are invaded (for it seems inevitable) Jean and Victoria will go to Yorkshire while I shall go with the Department to Droitwich.

9 June

With all this going on, meaning the rescue of our defeated army from the sands of Dunkirk by an armada of small boats, I was hailed from a smart-looking van in Margaret Street, 'Jack Wise, Modiste' painted in florid letters on the side. Was some moments recognising Jacob Weisz (I think that's how it was spelled), whom I had last seen in my rent-collecting days ripening bananas in a basement in Fournier Street. His job was now racing round the big stores replenishing stocks of cheap print frocks as they sold out. I asked after Adolf Kohn and he turned a thumb down. Cancer. Mrs Kohn now runs the warehouse off Hounds-ditch stacked with the said cheap print frocks. Jacob had married Becky. 'Boy,' he said, 'are they spending! Can't fetch it out of their handbags fast enough. Nice to see you.'

So much has happened but all I can think of at the moment is the thunderstorm raging all round me, and the downpour of hail and rain. This follows three weeks of heat. The lawn is cracked, the clay welded into iron – the spade bounces back from it. Then the first skirmishing breezes sent clouds of seeds into the air and now the earth is swallowing all it can.

At Broadcasting House, Defence Executive first called upon volunteers to patrol the building overnight in two-

hour shifts. Our engineers came back to their desks unshaven, in slippers, and comatose. My turn was to have
been the following Wednesday but because I have also
joined the Local Defence Volunteers (called 'the Parashots')
organised solely for the building's defence, I seemed likely
to get out of it. We drill in the Concert Hall with broom-
sticks, have inspections in which the same unlucky fellow
with long hair is repeatedly told to visit the barber's, and are
likely to serve no useful purpose whatever should Germans
appear in Upper Regent Street. A gesture, perhaps.

I didn't get out of night-patrol. Yesterday I found myself
at the core of the country's wireless-grid, guarding the Control Room and the precious cupboards containing the
apparatus that couples the system with the underground
post office cables, a loaded shot-gun across my knees. Steel
doors and spy-holes, soldiers in the foyer, gas-proof doors,
a scrupulous system of passes, crossed and uncrossed –
these are not enough. We also had self and Bird from the
Drawing Office at such guard-points, two hours on and
four off, over a twelve-hour day. The excitement, the
strangeness, the unreality, the walking into famous rooms
and discovering celebrities trying to snatch some sleep,
made the day memorable.

Our appearance in the canteen with guns and armlets was
impressive. However, the guns weren't loaded – cartridges
are inserted only on site, which is in the gallery overlooking
what used to be the 'In Town Tonight' theatre. I was glad
to get astride my Enfield at 9 p.m. After the dim, de-
vitalised Maginot Line atmosphere of the fortress, it was
like coming into another world. One would think that the
whole system was impregnable but no, Sir Stephen
Tallents, who must have a flat near, walked in by a side door
in pyjamas and dressing-gown and reached the boiler-room
without being challenged. Also, Bird and I were nominally
under an ex-Director of Television who walked round in a

trance – turned out that he had directed ballet. All the same, I am now a servant of the Crown, under military jurisdiction, with formal powers to kill. And that raised an issue for, although in my time I have shot rabbits and shot *at* pigeons, killing anything is so foreign to my nature that I should have to be hypnotised to kill people, even Germans. Which means that I must try to get into the RAMC or Signals.

At the office the atmosphere is irresponsible and feverish, even though we know that the work in hand has become even more urgent. De-centralisation is the principle behind the establishing of small 2-Kilowatt short wave transmitters north and south of London, with relay transmitters in the provinces and other 2 Kw's in old studio premises. To this end new men are being engaged. Bird is one. He has come straight from Shrewsbury. He had never so much as visited London before and reminds me of me in 1931 when I used to wander in a daze round side-streets. His ambition is to acquire a short wave communication set and he believes that the foundation of all matter is electrical. A strong, serious personality.

A week ago I watched a street cinema, contained in a van of which the engine charged the batteries for a projector, in aid of National Savings. It was a film of the Dunkirk operation, that is, the rescue of a large part of our army and some French from the sands of Dunkirk. Among those Yiddish tailors and foremen and button-makers (this was in Margaret Street) I became aware of a common anger: those muddied and exhausted men stumbling off gang-planks were the chaps one usually meets in pubs or walking the street with their girls. One hears accounts of sergeants swimming with wounded on their backs, a fisher-boy making the cross-Channel trip three times in a boat that had been holed by shrapnel and plugged with waste, of a 'once round the lighthouse' motor launch sunk by shellfire apparently in mid-Channel and finding itself in only five feet of water. Oddly enough, while cutting the front hedge at North Harrow I had heard the drumming of guns which could only have come from Dunkirk (as it turned out later) and called Amos from next door to listen. His comment was: 'Our turn next'.

Chalked up on a roadmender's barricade in Bolsover Street were the words: '*Sive* something *Brittanica* something *nunquam non paratus.*' Caesar's *Commentaries*, I shouldn't be surprised.

16 June

I think it was on Tuesday that, while I was wheeling the Enfield down the entry, Jean put her head round the kitchen door and said Italy had joined in. At midnight we were listening to Roosevelt describing this as 'a dagger in the back'. It's all very well making remarks like this from across the Atlantic – what are they going to do? Come in towards the end like last time and say they won the war?

The outstanding personal event of last week was that I was given a 5% cost-of-living rise and a further flat five bob a week for working a 48-hour week. Also the Bank Manager said that he could let me have a further £30 should I need it. The outstanding public event was the German invasion of Paris.

17 June

The future will tell, I daresay, but at this moment we are given up to gloom – almost. Now it is the French army that has capitulated: it has been rolled back from Belgium into Flanders, into Burgundy, into Normandy, into Paris, and through Paris, and now it has surrendered. Don't see what else it could do. That is all we know except that the octogenarian Petain has declared that the capitulation is more high policy than military. We fear that the navy has gone, too, and the air force, and the Maginot Line, and all the army's equipment. We fear that we are alone. We fear air raids this very night. Even so, we feel sure of ultimate victory, and it's not the silly confidence that's born of repetition and being told so, but a certainty born of a sullen sort of anger. Each tells the other about the navy and the army in the East, American aid, the nearness of Canada, the loyalty of Australia, Rhodesia, South Africa, the new government under Churchill. We remember that all Europe has been against us before and still we have come through. Underneath all these reassurances, a nameless dread.

I don't suppose the Guv'nor is typical, although he may be, of some. He is in a frightful state of nerves, hangs on the radio bulletins as they come round, and his whole body shakes when he tries to communicate his fears. Jean is much saner and steadier than me – more practical. So is her mother, who makes us laugh with her elaborate preparations to take to the Kodak shelters for the night. To Kodak's eternal credit, it has thrown open its deep, well-furnished and ventilated shelters to near neighbours.

Jack (Jean's brother), Mary (his wife) and Robert John (their 2-year-old) have come here for a week's holiday. We played 31's last night amid continual laughter. Everyone feels irresponsible, as though decision had been taken out of our hands. I don't feel exactly irresponsible but I have that inborn sense of fatality, of not worrying over things outside my control, that makes me seem carefree. I have done all I can to make my family secure and for the rest, I'll meet it when it comes.

Yesterday's news, except for the hard news, invariably full of rubbish – vain promises of fallen countries holding out to the last man, of fighting with spades, of retreating to fight again. Nobody believes it. In Britain it's a war of words, which reminds me that I am a very small part of it.

23 June

Spent last Friday on duty with a gun overlooking the Control Room. The shifts were to have been from 9 to 11 p.m. and from 3 to 5 a.m. but because the Germans came raiding the SE coast a 'yellow' was signalled, I was pulled out of bed in our 'dormitory' on the second floor, and at first was stationed outside an emergency door to which the public had access.

My fellow guard writes for radio. We talked about James Hanley and Christopher Isherwood, homosexuality, TV, and bombing raids. He has written two 'rather sad and depressing novels' which remain unsold. The first took him four years to write. I didn't let on that I had had three published because it would have silenced him. He says that religion and sex are the only things worth talking about but includes radio engineering in religion. He tells me to read Plato's *Symposium* and Franz Kafka's *The Castle*. It was a new experience for me to be asked by a stranger at four in the morning when I had had my first woman.

Otherwise the night was made memorable by the studio in which I slept, big, echoless, dim, and lifeless, with the deep immanent hum of engines within the walls; also by eating chocolate at midnight and drinking strong sweet tea in the restaurant at 3.45 a.m. together with police, soldiers, and mechanics; by my gazing for an hour at a pile of empty biscuit-tins; by my thinking as I dropped off at 1.15 a.m. of a German airman flying high up in the void of night above Southampton, his instrument-panel and the stars his only illumination.

On these occasions I have no fears for Jean and our baby if only because her mother lives only two hundred yards away. The house is as secure as I can make it and, short of having her with me in Broadcasting House, I can do no more for her.

On the Saturday morning, after a cold bath in the sub-

basement and a luxurious meal of grilled mackerel, I
attended drill in Beaumont Mews, Marylebone High
Street, where I had half an hour's broomstick drill, instruction in the mechanism of an army rifle, and ten rounds with
a small-bore. For some reason I excelled at shooting but
was a frightful duffer at drill, put to shame by my incompe-
tence just as I was in the playground at school when Pape
was drilling us.

France's collapse was at first terrifying but we have
grown used to the idea, particularly since Churchill's fighting speech on Monday night. At this moment we are waiting for news of the Armistice terms. (Mental picture of me
age 10 running down the back lane shouting 'Armistice!
Armistice!' and later asking Dad what the word meant.)
Our anxiety is the whereabouts and disposal of the French
fleet. Canadians and New Zealanders and Australians have
landed, swelling our army to one and a quarter million. But
what equipment was lost – what tanks, guns, and explosives
– during the retreat to Dunkirk!

30 June

All Thursday night I was on volunteer patrol against possible
sabotage with Cecil Madden (Producer of the first play
on television in this country). We had authority to enter any
room, demand anyone's pass. At 8.30 p.m. I was watching
the sun sink over Harrow and at 3.30 a.m. observing the
first streak of grey-green light over the Estuary, the barrage
balloons floating in the cool dawn air, the twinkling traffic
lights far down in Portland Place. We slept this time in a
screened end of the Drawing Room but as the other end was
occupied by visitors – a clique of French Staff Officers –
and a wireless receiver giving out the news in French, I rose
at 6.20 a.m. and took a Workman's home, returning to the
office about 2 p.m. We came across Norwegians (occupying
the august Council Chamber), Arabs, Greeks, Egyptians,

two laconic Americans, a Fire Squad going its rounds, news editors, electricians, two fitters dismantling part of the ventilation plant, a painter, Sir Stephen Tallents, a number of Overseas News editors, an announcer (English) 'hitting the mike', clusters of secret little studios each with its control room and microphone – I forget what else. We found 'Sprott's Folly', a narrow improvised staircase down which some bulky lady had failed to pass, an incredible cupboard that gave access to a maze of trunkings that dived into the earth, the deserted Control Room proper (note: discover the uses of all those grey cabinets for my next book on the early days of broadcasting), the roof, the Matron's room, a lonely typist afraid of mice, two girls on the PBX switchboard wrapped in rugs in easy-chairs within easy reach of the plugs, the library which I noted in passing was sloppily organised, with books all over the place in no sort of order – there was so much to remember and store away.

Cecil Madden told me among other things that I should find it useless to put in a radio play, or even an idea for one, as the acceptance thereof was at the discretion of a narrow clique who somehow all preferred their own productions to anyone else's. Some insight was given me into the tier upon tier of bureaucracy ruling within the organisation. He himself was a television man noted, among other things, for the nakedness of his chorines. Everywhere one meets such disconsolate TV staff sighing for the resurrection of 'the Palace' (Alexandra Palace) and 'Pig's Alley' (Swain's Lane). He knows Spanish, lived in Westminster, and spoke of meeting people like Vicki Baum, Somerset Maugham and Sinclair Lewis and his wife Dorothy Thompson. When at last I confided the secret of my books he said: 'Keep them secret, at least while the war's on. Don't for a minute think of trying to get in here. It'll kill any talent you have.' And he added a remark that startled me: 'I envy you.'

On Saturday morning I took drill again, shot ten rounds

and again excelled with nine bull's-eyes out of ten, and spent the next hour being taught how to take a gun away from a sentry. I tricked him by pretending to drop my guard and ask for a match. Also I got a smack on the jaw from a rifle-butt.

Our first air-raid alarm of the present cycle of alarms took place last Monday (I think). I heard Jean's heart beating within the sounding-board of the pantry's wooden walls. The child slept and played and slept again, all within this three feet of space otherwise occupied by shelves loaded with a bread-bin, sugar, margarine, and tins of this and that. I made tea, walked round, poked my head outside, and went back to bed ten minutes before the All Clear sounded. Joy F. visited us yesterday (now Mrs Lock) and told us a typical yarn that might have come out of Ireland. Her father went a bit queer when the Alert sounded, washed his dental plates, put on his boots, and gathered all his wife's furs out of a skip. Later on they heard a series of whistles which they took to be the All Clear but which turned out to be the old man snoring. They went to bed, nevertheless, but thought that the real All Clear was another warning and went downstairs again.

14 July, Sunday

I registered for military service on Saturday, having previously been warned by memo from the Executive that I was not, after all, in a reserved occupation. A frightful attack of asthma last night – I suppose, a subconscious reaction. Consciously I feel relief and only hope that I can get into some sort of corps that relieves and rescues rather than kills. Was wakeful till dawn, when we breakfasted, did our chores, and went back to sleep until 11.30 a.m. But I still feel half here. Jean says: 'Well, if Joy F. can manage, I can, and Stan's in the navy.'

16 July

As I said, I registered on Saturday; the As and Bs were called between 12.30 p.m. and 1 p.m. The Labour Exchange clerk simply took my name from my Identity Card, asked me about my education, preferences of duty, and nature of job. How was he to put down on the card he filled out that this man wasn't really a cost-clerk in the engineering division of the BBC but a novelist who was obliged to scribble the drafts of his books under a note-pad? So I didn't tell him. A column of men four abreast almost encircled the building, all looking very glum. The reason for my not being reserved is still a mystery: the odd thing is that, under everything, I didn't want to be reserved. With luck I might find my proper level in the army.

Every step one takes brings home the fact that we are not only at war, but in a corner. The fear of invasion hangs over every minute of the day. We hear of bombs shattering a house or two, of Hanley dog-race track being blown up, of Southend's nightly raids, but these rumours only serve to exasperate. It is the preparations for meeting an army among the fields around us, at home, that fill us with dread. The meadows beyond the Iron Bridge over the railway, where Jean and I wandered when engaged, on our way to Grimsdyke and Old Redding, are scarred with long trenches and mounds to prevent the landing of any planes and gliders. Also, in lieu of trees, stakes and poles have been planted. These preparations seem to have taken place overnight. Similarly with all the parks and playing-fields. Concrete gun-emplacements ('pill-boxes') have been created, or are being created, in tactical positions – I saw one behind a cricket-pavilion. Old Fords full of bricks are left by the wayside ready to be shoved broadside on into roads. Poor Laurence Kamm, the most scatterbrained of men, while driving home at 11 p.m. without his papers, was taken to the police station by an LDV with a fixed bayonet. The whole of the east coast as far as the Humber is said to be under military control, as is the length of the south coast. Passage in and out of this zone is forbidden. Cars and motor-cycles must be rendered useless when left parked. The army is buying up all motor-cycles of over 500 cc newer than 1936. Winston talks in a grim and powerful speech of fighting if need be through the streets of London and in the colonies. Letters from the north contain only hints of what is happening there because information must not be given away. The names on post offices, sign-posts, on railway stations and AA call-boxes have been obliterated. Steel helmets are carried by every other man. All the talk is of 'he's scratching his head how to get here', and 'he'll make use of the first fog.' That Channel, and what we owe to it!

Was talking last Wednesday to a little miner from Small-thorne ('Smaothun' in the vernacular – at school we had a couple of boys, twins, who came from Smallthorne) who had lost his leg through trench-feet in 1917, taken up court-shoemaking, and was now operating a small secret tele-phone exchange through which passed direct lines from the Ministries of War and Air, and the Admiralty. Also to a girl of about eighteen who was nursing a hand just healing from a wound caused while operating a capstan-lathe in a munitions-factory. She wanted a home of her own because she was sick of her parents' grumbling and quarrelling. Also to a knowledgeable fellow of parts whose business it was to keep the different broadcasting stations supplied with musical scores, and who had a passion for O'Henry.

My latest spy-thriller, *The Spy Who Died in Bed*, was sent off three weeks ago but I haven't heard what anyone thinks of it yet. A useless, old-fashioned book, seen in retrospect. Never mind, I'll build up to something new and big in the broadcasting-book.

6 August

After a twelve-hour LDV duty and a heavy meal (this meant leaving home at 7.45 a.m. and returning at 10 p.m.), I slept well and deeply until 7.30 a.m., the first time for a fortnight and feel unusually buoyant accordingly. Ten days ago I was down with asthma and now and then still feel that terrifying tightness after a burst of laughter or a short run.

Should have been on holiday this week but was asked to postpone it until next week. August Bank Holiday was of course a full working day. We made a good weekend, nevertheless, going as usual to a cricket-match on Saturday afternoon and afterwards to the tennis finals. At the last moment Jean and I decided to attend, in shifts, the Finals Dance, the one on duty of course looking after the baby. Jean went from 9 to 10.15 and returned saying that it had been dull. Then I went for an hour or more and returned to relieve Jean who brought back a mob of people to tea at 2.15 a.m. For some hours we forgot about the ever present threat of war and invasion.

Because Jean had found at the Club, of which we have been members for ten years or more, a small cluster of slim bored young girls and was not herself, as in the past, in the centre of things but was forced to dance four times with old Mr White, she considered herself done for – passée, a matronly curiosity from days gone by. She spent all Sunday morning shortening and ironing her smartest dress and when we took the infant to the Club in the afternoon was at pains to look cool and bored and to disregard the said slim girls.

15 August

Went for my medical at a Church Hall at Wembley, and found between thirty and thirty-five naked men disposed round its interior stooping, flapping their arms, even climbing and re-climbing a flight of four stairs leading nowhere. I passed through Grade IA together with a market-gardener until I came to the Chairman who was surprised that none of the seven specialists had asked about or discovered the asthma I mentioned. (He had remarked quite casually, as an aside: 'There's no reason why we shouldn't give you full marks, is there!' to which I had replied: 'Nothing, apart from the asthma.') A benevolent old dear in charge of chest and respiratory organs was asked to join us and put a stethoscope to my chest, which he did, afterwards declaring that he couldn't hear so much as the suspicion of a wheeze. I was bold enough to suggest that if they cared to attend me at eleven that night they would hear a wheeze or two. Corky supplied a certificate with the result that I am now graded IVD, with the feeble-minded and paralysed. Whether from relief or nerves or disappointment I was on the verge of tears when the Chairman passed me the green discharge certificate. He in turn was apologetic for doing so. Immense relief on Jean's part, but that same night by way of celebration I was up at 2 a.m. making tea and taking Ephedrin.

'Celebration'? Not the right word. I had had a sneaking hope that I would change my life for a bit, meet new people, live a new life.

18 August, Sunday

The week has ended in a burst of dog-day heat and sun. Last night we went to another tennis-dance. This time, with her hair newly set and in her nice new mauve dress, Jean found herself pursued as she used to be pursued. After dancing with his sisters, Keith came over and sat her on his knee, Keith being very much the cynosure in his Pilot's uniform.

All this is tittle-tattle when set against the week's raids, but even tittle-tattle has its place in times like these. In Harrow the sirens went three times. Victoria was already restless when the first sounded (Thursday, I think) and was

downstairs being comforted so we bundled her into the
pantry. Phyllis Anderson, with whom I had been playing
singles, was with us, and she too sat with us in the pantry.
The second occupied half an hour of Friday's lunch-hour,
when we were again at home, but we were scattered when
the third alert sounded. Victoria was with her grandmother,
which is something Jean tries to avoid. Jean pretends, for
Victoria's sake, that these Alerts are just another noise and
nothing to be afraid of, but her mother panics and races for
the garden shelter. Jean herself was this time shopping in
Wealdstone and reports that she and other shoppers flocked
to an inadequate shelter near the Bank. I was in Harrow
buying five shillings worth of Rynex at Boots. The siren
sounded from the top of an outsize drainpipe attached to a
Police Box opposite Woolworth's and fairly made the
ground and air shudder. Among the crowd of shoppers and
shop-girls streaming to the shelters behind the Granada
Cinema I felt a lump come to my throat. This was what we
had read about in H.G. Wells and what the reporters
had seen in Shanghai, Barcelona, and Rotterdam. Not the
least sign of panic. Prams, scooters, and bikes were left with
a helmeted Marshal outside the Shelter. Inside, children
were playing in a labyrinth of concreted, sterilised passages,
and girls were chatting with women whom ten minutes
before they had been serving with foundation-cream
or a pound of streaky bacon. There was even a woman
arrived, grumbling because she had been held up by
police who had ordered her to take cover elsewhere, to take
charge of the women's lavatories. So the reporters had been
wrong about their prophecies of air-raids in Britain – no
terror-stricken crowds fleeing for cover but a grumbling
lavatory attendant arriving late.

This must be the first time ever that an attacking air fleet
has met competent defences. Some time ago a newspaper
had come out with the headline: 'WHO'S TO BE OUR NELSON

THIS TIME?' and it almost looks as though we have found him, although I don't know his name. The papers treat the raids as they would a cricket-match: '144 for 17, Hurricanes stop play'. Last night Duff Cooper, in that quiet ironic voice of his, asked Hitler to come again and keep his promise of invading us. I think our attitude can justly be summed up in the retort of the second-former to the school bully: 'Come on and try.'

Meanwhile life goes on and my summer holiday is over. Victoria is scrambling about, talking her own language, growing molars, and making things difficult for us when we try to put her to bed. We left her to cry last night until 7.45 p.m., and it nearly broke our hearts.

23 *August, Friday*

Very early this morning a dull but resounding 'Who-omph!' sent me flying out of bed into Jean, who sleeps with the baby because of teething problems (or naughtiness, we can't decide which), just as another two 'oomphs' sounded. Jean thought they were thunder and was enjoying them, as she enjoys all thunderstorms, but on my swearing that they were AA guns she streaked into the pantry, baby, hot-water bottle, and cushions, inside two ticks. We were both wrong. One bomb had landed on the Herga Cinema, at which last Friday we had been watching *Beau Geste*, and the other live one on Barclay's Bank at the corner of Lockett Road and Wealdstone High Street. The third turned out to have been a time-bomb which caused two hundred yards of the High Street to be railed off this morning.

At the time we knew nothing of all this. Five minutes after we were all safe the Alert went and when they had stopped, police whistles blew up and down the street. From the back door I saw a solitary plane, my first glimpse of the enemy, caught up in a fistful of searchlights, which barely showed under a brilliant white moon. We surmise that one raider had become bottled up in the AA defences and had unloaded its burden of bombs, so that it was a pure fluke Wealdstone had happened to lie beneath. What was to us the major campaign of the war so far is described in the papers as 'minor aerial activity during the night'.

Yesterday for the first time the Germans tried shelling a convoy from the French coast. Also for the first time they shelled Dover, which must have memories of – was it Big Bertha? – that threw shells across the Channel in 1914/ 1918. New tactics. Italy has demanded that Greece renounce the British guarantee, which involves Turkey, which involves Russia. We may soon see a radical change in the war's strategy.

27 August
Bird of the Drawing Office had a letter from his father in Shrewsbury this morning saying that things were very quiet in those parts and he hoped Bird Jnr. wasn't being troubled too much by these sirens. Last week the remark would have been pointless but this morning it convulsed us. Bird himself had spent from 9.30 p.m. yesterday evening until 4.30 a.m. this morning (seven hours) in a public shelter in Harrow. By the Sunday night (25th) while on LDV duty I had done my normal 9 p.m. to 11 p.m. shift on sentry duty when the first siren went, three of which kept me up till 3 a.m. when my shift came round again. I was so utterly fagged that I went home and tried to sleep but could not, either before or after lunch. The siren went again about 3.30 p.m. but we heard no bombs or guns and at 4.30 p.m. I phoned Fletcher that I had slept till then (a gross lie) and didn't feel like going in again. For the rest of the day I pottered round vacantly, watering the seedlings for next year and in the evening fixing up the divan in the front room as a bed, with the solid oak bookshelf protecting it from the windows. At its head we placed Victoria's pram,

stripped of its handles.

Following the 9.30 p.m. Alert I slept most of the night on the divan, disturbed out of what would ordinarily have been the sleep of the dead by Victoria's snufflings and stirrings, the crump of bombs falling, the drone of enemy planes, and sharp ha-ha-ha of machine-guns high above our heads. Jean slept part of the time on the divan with me, partly under the stairs, and partly in her bed. Nothing is really clear about the night's proceedings: they are all a mixture of nightmare, of Victoria's sudden cry as a muffled 'Crump!' sounded close by, of the bark of the AA guns, of strange aerial clamour, of making tea, of changing beds, of watching the searchlight fingers rubbing their tips along the clouds, and of fervent unashamed prayer. I woke up in the little room upstairs, over the stairs, although goodness knows how I got there, and put my head out in expectation of seeing Harrow in ruins, but found nothing out of place. Neither post nor papers were delivered. At the office people arrived late, rubbing their eyes.

Today I have bought a camp-bed – and lucky, at that, because most camp-beds have disappeared from the shops – and shall sleep on it tonight with the back of the settee for protection, leaving the divan for Jean.

I was scared last night. Lying in one's bed, one feels hopelessly exposed and afraid. Perhaps one grows used even to this.

28 August

Last night we were not so scared, nor so disturbed, although four terrific 'whoomphs!' sounded about 4 a.m., shaking the windows, long after the second and last All Clear had sounded. In the mornings I greet Amos across the fence simply with a stare until one of us says: 'Noisy!' and the other says: 'Where were they?' to which the standard reply is: 'Sounded round the corner but I expect it was

Uxbridge.' He looks very grey these days. His school has large underground shelters and he tells me that the Head is just getting round to organising classes and lessons in them.

These Alerts and All Clears have the unique power to disorganise the life of every citizen within earshot such as this country has never known before. Sometimes they seem quite irrelevant although one has a pleasant feeling of relief when the All Clear sounds, as though officially we could relax. Another official note that one is prompted to suspect is the optimistic reports given in the News. Word of mouth differs from them considerably, as for example one of the engineers lately in Birmingham tells us that it has suffered a great deal of damage whereas no hint of any but small material damage has been reported in bulletins and papers. All right, the principle is not to keep the enemy posted but it also has the effect of not keeping *us* posted, and we want to know so that we can face what's coming. Similarly we heard suspiciously little about Monday's six-hour raid and we shall hear nothing of the various bombings of Uxbridge and its airfield. After the war we shall suffer a spate of information about wreckage, carnage, heroism, and fortitude. Or by then will everyone have grown tired of such tales?

I should have mentioned that while standing at the heart of Broadcasting House last Sunday and hearing the shrill wail of sirens I was given an unforgettable picture of the frustrations of the News staff in not being able to report what they know is of prime interest. I was in the BA Studio with my gun when the News people came trooping in because the Alert was wailing. They went to their jobs with studied indifference. Progress of the raid came down to us through a loudspeaker from a commentary on the roof. Even the typists, between intervals of typing from dictation, lit cigarettes as though lighting cigarettes were their religion. They were there to sift through and edit newstapes

from Reuters, the Press Association, and Exchange, Telegraph and News. A young woman of 20-odd, cigarette
drooping from her lip, lifted up a phone-receiver and
announced: 'Here's that young chap from Khartoum again,
wanting to know whether he'll be in time if he gives his
dispatch in now.' A voice from the other side of the room
said distinctly: 'Stuff Khartoum.' The real news was meanwhile coming down to us from the roof but they were
unable to report it.

3 September, Sunday

The raids persist, as indeed we knew they would, for we
gather that their effect is intended to be cumulative, but at
home we have not heard the crump of bombs since last
Friday night. Our arrangements are so organised that the
sound of the sirens only evokes a gesture of resignation. In
an attempt to prevent what happened not long ago, when
we swapped beds and cover all night through hoping to
obtain shelter and get some real sleep, we have so rational-
ised affairs as to divide the front (dining) room by the large
book-case which guards Jean and me against flying glass,
while theoretically Victoria sleeps under the table in her old
pram, now divested not only of its handle but also of its
wheels. In practice she doesn't like the situation at all and
sleeps with her mother on the divan while I sleep on the
camp-bed. This morning at a quarter to seven she was
awake enough to crawl over and pinch my nose and lay her
head on my shoulder emitting her idea of a hearty chuckle.
When the guns and bombs draw near we creep yawning into
the pantry, make tea, help Victoria suck barley-sugar, and
eventually creep back again. One has an impression of all
London and its suburbs leading similar lives. Last weekend
Bob Kieffer apologised to Victoria on behalf of his generation for this humiliating state of affairs.

By chance last week I was on the Central Line (Underground) and saw a mass of people camped out for the night, on the platforms. All very orderly, with helmeted Marshals in charge, family groups established in a sort of enclave with old people already lying down swathed in blankets, mothers making tea or brewing up soup (as I supposed) on camp-stoves, and small children watching the train, not really interested because they had got used to them. Some three feet had been left between them and the edge of the line for the use of passengers. Transform the tiled walls and advertise-ments into rock and one had a fair idea of what life must have been like in Neolithic times. The tunnels, passages leading to other lines, staircases, cut-throughs to the line going the other way, were all cavernous but made not so frightening by the chatter of voices and obvious mateyness, just as it must have been in those days.

As for Broadcasting House, we have already had today two spells of one hour each in the basement shelters. The evening papers speak of a terrific air-battle over Kent and the estuary. These air combats are indescribable – the fearful odds, the issues involved, the audacity – they are as epic as the tale of the *Revenge*, the Armada itself. Where Nelson had shattered Napoleon's hopes of invasion by a victory at sea, so now it appears that a later 'Trafalgar' is taking place in the air. These battles happen every day. Only the numbers of the vanquished and casualties vary, and even their ratio is fairly constant: around three or four of theirs to one of ours. We are after all on home ground. The papers and bulletins are hard put to write up the same heroism in different words, with different details and from different angles. Who would have imagined heroism be-coming monotonous and imminent death routine, or the process of devastation needing sauce to make it interesting?

Eden today talks of 'invasion not being by any means a danger yet past'. Perhaps this is a hint that invasion might after all be just that?

10 September

I am scared stiff that the typescript of my spy-thriller, the only one in existence, typed by Jean, may now be smouldering in the fires which, according to the 8 a.m. bulletin, were started last night in Paternoster Row. Too near St Paul's, too. I proposed to Jean in St Paul's – well, it was the most crucial step yet in both our lives and worthy of the surroundings. Luckily she said yes and by an extraordinary chance I had the engagement ring with me, so that was that.

Following what must have been the most dangerous and was certainly the most terrifying weekend of our joint lives we have emerged unscathed and with a feeling of triumph because our nerves are still normally responsive.

It began on the Friday night when I was roof-spotting on Broadcasting House, being one of the first to do so. The sirens were sounding so many times and the alerts lasting so long that people were spending more time in their shelters than at their desks. It was therefore decided that they should go down only when warned of imminent danger by a roof-spotter. I saw the new moon sink below the horizon, a glare over the estuary which was rumoured to be an oil-tanker on fire, bunches of searchlights spring up and vanish over different quarters of the horizon, bursts of shrapnel appear in the form of sinister little smoky flashes, and finally little bunches of flares appear in the sky, dropped by an almost inaudible plane which set out over the river and toured the outskirts via (I guessed) Dalston, Highgate, Cricklewood, Bayswater, and vanished towards Kingston-on-Thames. From one of the untidiest spectacles in the world, the roof-tops of London, under the glare of the dripping flares, became one of the most majestic. At the time we thought less of the spectacle than of the danger, but nothing happened.

The bombers followed the next afternoon (Saturday) and it was this raid which so far constitutes our greatest defeat. I was at home by then and saw the sky glowing in the south-east. A group of uneasy people were watching from the Iron Bridge which, being over the railway lines heading north and south, commanded the best view. Beyond a violent flaming sky, layered by banks of cloud, nothing could be seen, however. This turned out to be the notorious Docks fire of 7 September and was far brighter than the memorable Crystal Palace fire in 1936 which we saw from the top of Shoot-up Hill, Cricklewood, taking place on the other side of London. Promiscuous bombing did not occur until Sunday night when hospitals and cinemas and shelters, the Edgware Road and Whitechapel High Street, alike suffered terribly. That Saturday night, although we were roused time and again by the dull reverberations of falling bombs and the cannonading of anti-aircraft guns, we were only frightened by three bombs, which fell among the fields of Hall's Farm, ten minutes away.

Two notes in passing, the first that when bombs fall near Jean tells the baby so that she shouldn't be frightened: 'Oh, golly, that was a big one! I bet you – I bet you we get even *bigger* ones.' But how much she is kidded I don't know. The other aside is that when Hall's milk roundsman knocked on the door next day he said: 'My ruddy 'orse's all wore out with runnin' rahnd and rahnd.'

To continue. On the Sunday night we knew that we were for it because a tremendous barrage broke out about 8.10 p.m., all the way from Uxbridge to Wembley to Northolt, dull reddish-yellow flashes stabbing the mid-air. And again (asthma was troubling me and the din woke Victoria, who would not be pacified) we heard the racket of London being bombed. One terrific crash fetched us out of bed but we never found out what happened, and it was not repeated. On my way to work by motor-bike, taking the back streets, I was compelled to go out of my way because of craters at Neasden, where also a concrete pavement was standing on end. More craters at Cricklewood, where a poor-class house had been completely demolished, and along the Edgware Road. Here I saw two refugees who might have walked straight off the front page of the *Daily Mail* – sweaty, blowsy women with disordered hair, still grinning, although possibly they had missed by inches the death that had overtaken their friends and families.

But the greatest devastation that I saw was at Chiltern Court which now looks like an East End tenement, its windows blown out, its middle ravaged by one bomb whose twin had landed plumb on Tussaud's Cinema, scattering masonry over the Euston Road, causing Tussaud's itself to collapse, turning the adjoining mews into a shambles of bricks, coping-stones, furniture, glass, and human and wax flesh. Even the large Crown Estate residences in the Outer Circle of Regent's Park, a whole arc of them, had spewed out their glass as far as the gardens. But complete, almost matter-of-fact calm in the way the police steered traffic round the debris, the firemen stood by, the Civil Defence in steel helmets stood round a WVS mobile canteen, the blue-clad heavy-mob (Heavy Rescue) were rigging up block and tackle. This was the after-the-party scene. What sort of hell it must have been a few hours earlier is anyone's guess.

Jean and I have now finally come to rest on camp-bed and couch in the drawing-room (at the back) while Victoria lies snug in her carry-cot behind the chimney breast and protected by a book-case. As a result we spent a good night last night, heedless of the planes which were ranging up and down the Thames Valley. I am to hang wire-netting over the French windows and meanwhile I push the single mattress against them, backed by another bookcase, backed by an arm-chair.

We are either wise or lucky. Fletcher hasn't slept before 2 a.m. for a week, Mrs Coleman and Clarke could not reach their desks yesterday because of bombed railway-tracks, the typists are really sick with fatigue and fright. Something's got to give – these conditions can't last.

11 September

Breathing not so good – aspirin, Ephedrin, and Rinex maintain a fluctuating normal.

Last night we again slept well although according to report London suffered the worst raid of the war. Bird and Duffield were on LDV duty, with Bird actually in the gallery overlooking the Control Room, when a description relayed from the roof of events outside was interrupted by a terrific concussion immediately followed by a flickering and then total extinction of all lights. Typewriters, talking, even the glowing of cigarettes, all ceased. Then in three minutes the emergency diesel engines started up, the lights came on, and life gradually began again. A 1000 lb aerial torpedo had landed on the roof of the White House by Great Portland Street Station in Euston Road.

Fires all over London. (There was even one in Miss Baker's back-garden which she put out 'with two shovelfuls of soil'.) Regent Street today is barred to wheeled traffic because Piccadilly Circus has copped it – how badly we don't know. Bird swears that Broadcasting House shook like a trap with a rat inside it. He has other misty recollections of drinking cold milk in the morning, by candlelight, with the head of the department, who was attired in pyjamas and dressing-gown. Also of sleeping beside the artists' lifts in the basement and being stepped over all night. The Concert Hall was packed with sleepers. The usual crop of rumours, e.g. that Regent Street and Bond Street are sacked and burnt (but I walked up one and down the other this lunchhour and noticed nothing out of place, except some windows); also that Churchill had given the Germans a twelvehour ultimatum to have Berlin vacated before it was laid in ruins – strange that a grocer at Bletchley in Buckinghamshire should have heard the same rumour.

The Guv'nor is speechless with a raging cold while even Jean, unusually, has the snuffles, both by-products of the blitz.

Another by-product has been the avenue's gas alert. Mrs Sowerby at No 62 first detected it and it was later commented on by a passer-by, unidentified. Result, two Gasboard vans, a number of officials with their noses to the ground looking mystified, and the appearance of the police warning households to put out all naked flames, whether those of a match or pilot-light or whatever. Half an hour later Mrs Sowerby says: 'Yes, that's where the smell's coming from' and points to the wooden fence dividing her estate from that of the Lindfields. Turns out that Mr Lindfield, neat and scrupulous as ever, had been creosoting his side of the fence.

Well, it demonstrates how quick off the mark the services are these days, and it has also given the neighbourhood something to laugh about in times not notoriously amusing.

16 September

Although I had been able to get a gallon of petrol on the side (i.e. without coupons) I went up by train so as to be able to drive up at a later date should the trains be thrown out of action, as has happened with the Southern Railway. Waterloo, for example, has been shut down for some days and a shot-down Messerschmidt has fallen inside Victoria Station. Although crowded, the train was roughly on time. All on board were smiling, also the soldiers one met, the porters, and the passers-by in the street, with a grand air of suppressed joy. A fair half of an invading air fleet was yesterday shot down ('littering the suburbs' as the papers say). In all we are told that 185 were destroyed with a loss to ourselves of only 25. The figures are incredible. We wonder whether superior design and workmanship, or the fact that

the battle was fought over home ground, are enough to
account for a seven to one victory. Myself, I think that the
British genius for piracy and improvisation is the root
cause. The exploits depend upon the individual and the
Englishman was always an individualist and loses interest
when the thing becomes routine and anybody's concern.
Another outstanding example of this same genius was given
by a squad of Royal Engineers under Lieutenant R. Davies
who removed a one-ton unexploded bomb from Dean's
Yard, St Paul's. Using special tackle because the eight-foot
projectile in its passage into the earth had been worn
smooth, they bore it off at full speed through streets cleared
by the police to Hackney Marshes and there detonated it,
making a crater 100 ft deep. I hope he gets all the medals he
ever wanted.

A tremendous row all last night, that is, from 11 p.m. to
5.30 a.m., mostly from AA guns. Rumour has assigned a
brace of naval guns to Belmont overlooking Stanmore and
perhaps it's these that make the bathroom door creak from
three miles away. Time-bombs have become a major nuisance. (In fact these were mostly 'duds'.) Fletcher's family
moved at five minutes notice because of one, and anywhere
along the road one is liable to meet a barrier and a diversion
sign. Staff from Twickenham talk of hearing a bomb
scream down and land not with an explosion but with a
thud.

In Foley Street W.1. I saw the result of one such bomb,
which had crashed whole into the cellar of a 3-storey house
and two hours later gone off, neatly demolishing just that
house and no other. When I saw the ruins, undergarments
were still hanging from the ledges of houses opposite.

Everyone has tales to tell of their being bombed, seeing
planes brought down, hearing guns in the city, taking re-
fuge in public shelters, and watching the little incidents
which go to make the history of a city in extremity. I was on

duty all Saturday and even my receptive powers weakened. One story stands out above the others and I will store it here.

Apparently the bonded warehouse of a former distillery lies beneath the platforms of Waterloo, now empty of casks, and hung with festoons of pale fungus and cobwebs. The Southern Railway opened it up last Monday after the large-scale night attacks began. Within two days the custom had established itself of queuing for a night's shelter with mattresses, bags of food, vacuum-flasks, and blankets. A woman carrying a small baby came down the steps. Fairly well spoken, nice clothes, but destitute. She had left her home at Dartford during the day to go shopping, taking the baby with her. On her return she had found nothing but a smoking ruin where her home had been, with a rope round it. Rather than accept the offer of shelter she had set out to seek her husband who was on a 48-hour shift in Westminster. She had pushed the pram as far as Waterloo, found herself caught in a raid, and run for shelter with the baby, leaving pram, vegetables, groceries, and handbag by the roadside. She was now hungry, and so was the baby. While she sat down to feed the baby, two volunteers went out in mid-raid under showers of shrapnel to retrieve the pram. They were laughing when they came back although their errand had (literally) been fruitless, because groceries, greengroceries, and handbag had vanished – stolen. However, they had brought back the pram and the baby went into it, and enough food was subscribed to feed the mother.

At 1 a.m. the mother confessed that the baby had to have a supplementary meal because he was the survivor of twins and a weakling. The two volunteers walked among the others in the shelter asking for a tin of Cow and Gate or Libby's and, when they had got it, they ran upstairs to the platforms, found a canteen serving tea, sterilised a coffeepot, and made a meal for the baby according to prescription. The baby was fed and went to sleep. The last incident was also memorable. The baby stirred in its sleep and like all restless babies began to whimper 'He-he-he-he!' when a soldier lifted his boot and pushed it against the pram and rocked it, sending it to sleep again.

The mother said: 'Oh, darling, if you only *knew* how many people are trying to help you!'

16 September

At this moment a policeman is knocking at the doors of the houses opposite Broadcasting House (in Bolsover Street) bidding their occupants leave because a time-bomb (or 'impendiary' as it is called) is lying somewhere at the back. All the stallholders of Great Titchfield Street, the bakers, the fruiterers, the invisible menders, and families with babies, are similarly trooping away. I saw an old woman sitting on two mattresses and holding a dog while a taxi drew up behind her and carried off all the loaves from the bakery against which she was resting. An incoherent, unhappy street-vendor of 'toilet requisites' went up the street with his barrow shouting his defiance, or perhaps it was only nonsense. In Langham Place I had to step over blocks of masonry from the bombed pinnacles of the Langham Hotel. New chips have appeared on the façade of Broadcasting House, the Director General's office windows are out, and an enormous crater has been made in Great Portland Street, immediately outside what had been the great Boswell's house. Not far off, the husk of a house is still dripping from its sprinkler valves. Flakes of glass were lying in heaps down Regent Street much as the snow lay in heaps this last February – as it seems, an age ago. The windows of the Galéries Lafayette, Hamley's, Jaeger, Dickins & Jones, are all blown out. Outside the Ford showrooms just off the Circus craters have laid bare pipes and conduits.

But there you are, while roof-spotting from the top of Broadcasting House, I was thinking that, after all, only minor damage had been done. The spires still point, the Middlesex Hospital still stands, and the huddled houses still give out smoke from their chimneys. When aeroplanes are overhead Bentinck House suddenly seems less a substantial structure than a pack of cards of which every other space is occupied by glass. Now, in the evening, the houses are all emptied of people, the cobblers have gone, the blowsy women no longer lean gossiping over window-sills but are probably – undoubtedly – gone to shelters with their canaries and mattresses, still gossiping.

To get to Broadcasting House I had to thread my way through streets barred to traffic and littered with débris. The front entrance is now blocked off and the west (Concert Hall) entrance is the only one in use. The Concert Hall is a mess and littered with 'boys' rehearsing, with staff cleared out of Brock House, with mattresses and blankets and pillows, with old newspapers and paper packets and even with milk bottles. And once even smoking was forbidden here! Some of the Langham Street windows (of Broadcasting House) are shattered and about a square half-mile surrounding the building is roped off and evacuated. It looks even more like a fortress, splintered and scarred but not substantially damaged, unlike the Langham Hotel which has tumbled its top bedrooms into the street.

But even so, no sign of panic or public disorder. The police are in full control. Once the high excitement of racing from doorway to doorway is over, dodging shrapnel and expecting one's steel helmet to protect one – actually, no more adequate to protect the head from those sizzling, razor-sharp fragments than a hare's foot – and the fear from hearing the scream of a descending bomb, a period of depression sets in. Have noticed it in myself, a sinking of the spirits and listlessness. I daresay prolonged exposure to such dangers may have some lasting effect. It's a period of every man for himself, as witness the rush for the shelters, but it's interesting that *in* the shelters everyone becomes matey, offers cigarettes, chats, even fetches tea from the canteen for someone else. No question of not surviving the bombing, which is regarded not with heroism or wringing of hands but as a colossal nuisance which must soon end. The smallest sign of hysteria, if that's the right word, rested in the word 'positively' in a chalked notice on a board (of which the reverse side read 'Fresh Fish'): 'Positively No Entrance'. Ordinarily 'No Entrance' would have been quite sufficient.

The departmental head has just announced that of all the engineering departments, ours is to be evacuated with all practicable speed to Droitwich. This is because the installation of those small transmitters is regarded as tactically important and the work is simply not being done because of the constant disruption, tiredness of engineers, difficulty in getting to work etc.

As for me, I am to go home and await instructions. Another corner to turn!

18 September

I am now at home, half wondering whether indeed I shall be called to Droitwich or politely turned off. All yesterday I spent parcelling the department up, ready for the removal to the bare huts waiting for us at Droitwich. Long talk with Jean, conducted in a half-feverish state while doing something else – should I in any case tell the BBC I prefer to see it out at home? The dread of unemployment still hangs over us. I doubt if I shall ever be rid of it. Should I go, would Jean bring the baby to join me, would she live with her mother, would she go to Newton Longville, near Bletchley in Buckinghamshire, where her parents have a week-end cottage? Reference to the map shows that Droitwich is not

more than seventy miles from Bletchley, not an impossible
week-end journey on a motor-bike. We can't make up our
minds. Above everything is the problem of her and the
baby's physical safety. I find in myself a sneaking desire to
see the inside of a transmitting station, for the sake of the
book on broadcasting I shall someday write. An invasion by
the Germans, of which there is increasing talk and increasing scepticism, would change the plans of everyone.

19 September

Yesterday was unforgettable. Bombs had dropped on a few
of the big Oxford Street stores and traffic was diverted
along lanes and up side-streets like New Cavendish Street,
which all the same was strewn with glass. Our own narrow
Bolsover Street became as thronged with traffic as Oxford
Street in normal times when the All Clear went and people
emerged blinking and sleepy-eyed out of their shelters,
most of them carrying rugs, pillows, blankets, and
shopping-bags stuffed with what was left of their suppers.
One side of Bolsover Street had been blown out but Bentinck House suffered the loss of only three panes of glass.
Bird and I climbed to the roof (of Bentinck House) to see
what we could see and found to our amazement the front
end of the chassis of a London bus – the curved lump of
iron, that is, on which the weight of the bus rests. There it
rested, already rusting, having been blown over the rooftops some nights ago.

Drove my bike round by Marylebone and Portman
Square because of traffic diversions caused by time-bombs.
Two such landed among the flats on the east side of Broadcasting House, obliging the Exec. to rail off the east corridors for a time.

The Concert Hall was a scene from Hogarth. A broadcast
by two pretty accordionists and full band was in progress in
the middle, in one corner the Cash Department had estab-

lished itself and next to it was a girl on a mattress, fast asleep. Part of the Features and Drama had appropriated another corner – they are going to Bangor, North Wales, I am told. Mountains of mattresses. All the tiers that had formerly held seats were flooded with girls in overcoats waiting to be evacuated. Messengers were eating apples, the Despatch Manager was looking gloomy as, with arms folded, he leaned against the east wall surveying it all, and in all that howling chaos two earnest women were beseeching silence for the broadcast. It looked like a shipwreck – like Bognor foreshore in August – like Burslem Wakes Week.

21 September, Saturday

I daresay that I ought, like Pepys, to be 'much terrified in the nights, nowadays, with dreams of fire, and falling down of houses', but in fact we have all slept well these last two nights. This morning I spliced a new shaft on a broken spade, cut the privet-hedge for the last time this year and wired a frame for the honeysuckle, tidied up the front garden and side passage, found a new foot-rest for the Enfield, and am now at my desk working out plot. Very quiet here last night but the wrecking of London continues. We are beginning to wish (if I am to believe Amos) that the invasion *would* take place so that a decision might be made one way or the other. Irresponsible thinking, perhaps, but at least if it happened it would avoid having both countries laid waste.

24 September

Yesterday motor-biked up to town, chiefly to collect my wages but partly to find out what damage had been done, and partly to find out what my section is up to. No instructions yet for me.

In the streets, the same air of unreality. Waitresses are

preoccupied, shop-girls talk excitedly to one another while serving, the crowds generally are wide-eyed, silent, and slow-moving. The worst sight of all was the wrecked and gutted John Lewis's building in Holles Street, off Oxford Street. Gaunt girders already rusting enclosed here and there by unwilling masonry, ruined and blackened walls rearing crumbled tops out of shapeless débris, the whole street heaped with masonry from which – last touch of realism – a thin plume of blue smoke was still spiralling. Hose pipes were still snaking down Oxford Street, fizzing with water from bursts due to flying glass. Only one police-man looked on, behind the newly erected barrier, disin-terestedly watching a couple of salvage men. The fire was out, there was nothing more to be done. It was yesterday's news.

The imposing corner of Peter Robinson's overlooking Oxford Circus had thrown its façade onto the pavement but the gaping hole (in the masonry) made the building seem merely naked and not wholly destroyed. After the calamity at Lewis's it was just a pity.

The 'emergency beds' situation in Broadcasting House is now under control. Instead of people lugging mattresses to wherever they could find a peaceful corner to sleep in, beds are now numbered and bookable, ladies here and gentlemen there kind of thing. Makes one wonder what's been going on, especially since complaints have been raised about the girls one meets in the corridors at night, attired in kimonos, bright blouses, and wearing mules more suitable for the bedroom than for those august corridors. The Concert Hall is still thronged with refugees – blokes and lassies and even executives waiting for someone to tell them what is to happen to them. For all I know, some may have been rendered homeless. The Chief Defence Officer has been issued with a summons for knocking down a fireman who was just coming off duty: the war has gone to his head and as an ex-military man he expects military discipline.

Today's funny story concerns the blowing of a whistle at 4.30 by the contractors for building the shelter going up outside Broadcasting House. It was relayed as an alarm by my old acquaintance, the one-time producer of TV ballet, who is now CO Home Guard, with the result that all and sundry scurried for shelter.

29 September

Somebody must have learned that I drove a motor-cycle – after all, I park the old Enfield in full view of other employees at the back of Bentinck House – for I was called up to Broadcasting House and given the job of driving a 348 cc Panther combination, straight off the assembly-line, between London and Islip, a village of about three hundred inhabitants on the far side of Bicester. Transpires that one or more departments have been evacuated to Islip's manor-house so that records and correspondence have to be carried daily between them and Broadcasting House. In the last three days I have travelled 504 miles, mostly at fifty or sixty m.p.h. On the Tuesday night I had the horrors imagining myself driving this novel form of vehicle up the Stockwell Road between ruined houses and skirting craters. In fact this happened. First there was an Alert while I was inspecting the vehicle at the depot, which sent us all to the shelter, and then I was given ten minutes tuition before I set off. Driving a combo calls for quite a different technique from driving solo but by dint of driving slowly I got used to the foot-change (the Enfield's gears are changed by means of a flick of the thumb, much as with bicycles) and the twist-grip accelerator, and beyond touching someone else's wing at some traffic-lights I have not yet come near an accident. I must say that I was scared because machinery doesn't obey me as it obeys, for example, my father-in-law. As for craters, there were so many that traffic wasn't even diverted round back-streets but skirted the holes as best they could. Came across one without so much as a rope round it.

Arrived at Broadcasting House at 5 p.m., I still had to go to Bicester and back, delivering files and correspondence at both ends. Reached home this side of eleven o'clock. A secretary had been kind enough to warn Jean, who had got the water hot for a bath and made a meal. Roads fairly empty and no obvious signs of war until, on the return journey, one found the empty windows of the Outer Circle in Regent's Park. The weather has been fine, even warm, and once I had got used to the feel of the bike I found myself enjoying the experience.

A land-mine floated down by parachute onto the Kodak playing-fields just over the houses opposite and rendered us homeless. It was Jean and I who had found it. Over the week-end a captured Messerschmidt had been put on show, sixpence to view, a shilling to sit in the cockpit. Jean and I had turned up first thing – were indeed the first customers because I had to go to work and the plane was only just round the corner at the top of the street. On leaving, Jean asked the gatekeeper: 'Is that tub-shaped thing with the parachute attached part of the show?' To which he replied: 'What tub-shaped thing? I don't know anything about a tub-shaped thing. I've been on fire-watch all night.' Ten minutes later the fun began. The police arrived at the double and turned the whole street out of doors, advising them to leave doors and windows wide open and then to make themselves scarce while the bomb was de-fused. While I went to work, Jean took the baby to some cousins in Kenton. Jean's mother is taking the raids badly and re- turned in a panic to her cottage at Newton Longville. Someone came and removed fuse and detonator and here we are back home again.

6 October

That interlude is over. In one week I travelled 1021 miles but now I have been given a one-way ticket to Droitwich. The BBC's generosity doesn't extend to paying for tickets for wives and babies. Yesterday I motor-cycled over 200 miles and then had to go on to Clapham to leave the Panther and collect my Enfield. It now seems as light and erratic as a scooter. Got lost among the interminable South London tramlines for not a place-name appears anywhere. I went through what must have been Balham and Tooting until I came to the recognisable streets of Mortlake, where I passed my old firm before taking a road I knew all too well.

Locally, several people were killed in Edward Road, immediately across Kodak playing-fields, and a tremendous crater has appeared at the back of an empty house in Pinner Park Gardens, not far from the home of Jean's parents. This happened on Monday night. On Thursday night Holmdene Avenue, in which stands my first home in these parts, was spattered with incendiaries, while the next road, Priory Way, got a high explosive. But all the same, a high explosive among these newish dormitory dwellings isn't the same as a high explosive on John Lewis's. On my motor-cycle round I heard of bombs being dropped on the lonely fields of Aylesbury, Kings Langley, and Bovingdon. At this moment a raider is overhead, above the low grey clouds. Several explosions sounded this morning, one so near as to send me scampering from the garden into the cover of the pantry.

Jean takes these unusual happenings quite calmly, I suspect out of regard for the baby. We find our knees shaking after a near explosion but recover quickly enough – unlike her mother who was with us during the Monday night raid and misbehaved herself as no adult likes to misbehave. Our plans for the future are vague but taking shape. Jean may spend a night at her mother's (although in the latter's present frame of mind that won't be much of a rest cure) or go to Newton Longville, or with luck I may be able to find rooms for her at Droitwich. One lives from day to day and she will not by any means be the only Government widow – this afternoon I met nice Mr Marsh much distressed because he is to go to Blackpool. When I asked what was happening to Mrs Marsh he waved his arms and said: 'She wants to stay in her own home but I ask her, with these Germans coming over?' Our position exactly.

7 *October*

Jean and I both came to the same conclusion at the same time, over breakfast. She said: 'I don't want to leave my home, Georgie,' and I said hastily because she wasn't far off tears: 'Neither do I. Let's not. I'm not bound to the BBC for all eternity.' Somehow we always arrive at the same conclusion about the same moment. But I must confess that whereas with Jean not leaving home is the whole reason, with me it's only part. The excitement of London under bombardment is one thing but rural Worcestershire is another. The job itself is chiefly copying orders in triplicate and making the relative entries in a ledger, plus the high excitement of being in charge of the stationery cupboard. Is this all I can do in time of war? Good God! But I've seen the homeless in the Underground, walking the streets with their pathetic belongings, and camping out in railway stations. Apart from the Salvation Army, who looks after them? The Housing Department of the respective Borough Council? If so, does it want men? Why can't I make people my business instead of ledgers?

Jean said: 'All the same, we've got to think of Victoria,' and I said: 'I'm rather stuck with the job. It's a tram I can't get off. They won't let me go.' Jean said: 'Try it for a bit and if things get too bad here I'll join you.' I said: 'I don't want to leave you,' and she said: 'I don't specially want you away from me, either, but that's how it would have been if you had been called up.'

That's roughly how the conversation went although no true record of any conversation can ever be made (unless by Henry James) because the subtleties are lost. Shall bike it to Droitwich and not use the BBC's one-way ticket. With a motor-bike I feel less of a prisoner.

9 October

This is written in the back bedroom of a Council House in Chequers Lane, Wychbold, which is the village on the main road from Droitwich to Birmingham, near the transmitting station. A strong westerly gale has been blowing all day, beating on the windows of the long army-hut which is to become the department's office, threatening to blow down the two 500-foot masts upon us in spite of their lacework of stay-wires and drags. We are high up here, in a field among many fields, with a view of distant spires and woods, arable and ploughed, green and red. A feeling of relief is abroad, even of holiday, as we ride up and down on the push-bikes given to us by the Corporation and lunch and tea together in the transmitting-station's canteen. My own room is speckless, and for supper I was given a slice of ham the size of a boot-sole.

But all the comforts of the lodging and the safety in which we work are a vanity when, walking up the lane at night, I hear a child cry.

My landlord gets up at 4.30 a.m. to travel to the Austin works at Birmingham, where he is a storekeeper. He is back home about 4.30 p.m. and sleeps a little before walking to the Crown for a pint. He says he feels unwell if he doesn't get that pint and he may be right because he works seven days a week. At 9.30 he goes back to bed. Mrs D. is just as ugly and tiny as a goblin. Her eyesight is poor and she has no interests outside cooking and keeping her home bright, making woollen rugs and knitting. In emergency the Crown will take her on as a chambermaid, cook, or waitress, but she doesn't like to leave her home and looks for excuses to refuse.

14 October

My chief concern, now that the office is in full swing again and likely to stay here, is to find a home for Jean and the infant. But because the engineers have been here before me, homes are as easy to find as jobs pre-war. But I must get those two out of Harrow. We learn that St Mary's spire has been toppled, that Colindale Underground station has been put out of action, and that a bomb has contrived to land on a Piccadilly escalator. One begins to see why in these parts the war is treated as a rather unpleasant newspaper serial. Have answered advertisements and toured the countryside on the bike, as also the residential quarter of Droitwich. Five of the engineers, and my immediate boss Fletcher, are likewise on the prowl.

Meanwhile Jean's temperament remains true. She appeared to take my departure calmly, saying that she had Victoria to look after and her mother not far away, but I had a tearful letter on Saturday complaining that these meant very little without her husband.

The cycle rides have brought me to prospects of quite incredible loveliness. The fleeting season, the sudden rows of trees, the twisting lanes, the steep dales and rounded summits, the half-timbered cottages and farmhouses, are a far cry from the toppled towers of Oxford Street.

I've just heard that the next fellow to drive the Panther got himself killed outside King's Langley while trying to keep to the schedule set for him by the Executive. I myself had one or two narrow shaves but the worst that happened to me was an official ticking-off by some faceless bigwig or other for not keeping to the schedule.

18 October

Hunting for houses in an area where all vacant property has long since been picked up by Adjutants' wives, Station engineers, and Birmingham commuters gives one a home-phobia: one looks at houses only as things to be coveted, at sheds as convertible property, and at railway-carriages as possibilities. McN., the deputy head, talks of 'comman-deering' a humble cottage from its quite inoffensive owner. Others spend their mornings phoning round and making sudden excited excursions. Fletcher scours the countryside and comes back with news of farmhouses with a pump in the garden and the closet out of sight letting rooms at fifteen bob each. As for me, I have found a lodging, albeit depen-dent on the whims of a slightly deaf, oldish, spinster, schoolteacher. Although the ad in the paper mentioned Saturday afternoon I went on the Friday evening in pouring rain and was obliged to wait half an hour with steaming trousers while the lady interviewed someone else. Then I unmasked the whole battery, my young wife's sorrow at parting from me, the patriotic aspect of admitting a family moved from its home in the national interest, and the clinching argument that my baby was being bombed. Mind you, the unspoken argument was the strongest, namely, that if she didn't let her rooms on her terms, she would be obliged to take someone in on the Billeting Officer's terms. Newish house, all conveniences. The others are incredu-lous, and the newspaperman shook my hand by way of congratulation.

20 October, Sunday

This morning I went to make beds with my new landlady, borrowed a cot, made things right as could be, all the time assailed by the hideous doubt that in coming to Droitwich and taking over part of this lady's house I was making a mistake that I should come bitterly to regret. Also I was given an intimation of the same operation being repeated a hundred thousand times by other evacuees to places like Blackpool, Rhyl, Newcastle-on-Tyne, and so on.

Posts very unreliable. Have not had a line from J. since Wednesday, and the parcel she posted on Tuesday has still not arrived. I wonder if Victoria would ever come to know the magnitude of the events which are bringing her away from her home so that she can sleep undisturbed.

27 October, Sunday

Jean left Paddington while a loudspeaker was announcing that enemy planes were at that moment directly overhead. So at least the reason for getting away was reinforced. The two of them arrived two hours late, thoroughly exhausted. I shan't easily forget the cameo of Jean dropping her case on the platform of Droitwich's darkened station while Victoria clung to her shoulder. I felt my heart lurch for they *looked* like refugees. Now Jean has recovered some of her stability and is studying to make herself agreeable to a stranger in the stranger's home, a task she doesn't take kindly to. Our home is to be let furnished so that my lovely leeks, carrots, parsnips, and artichokes will all be enjoyed by strangers.

The bombing is more intense (Jean tells me), the disorganisation more widespread, the devastation of fire and high explosive persisting. New Street Station, Birmingham, and Euston Station are the latest to suffer. But then every morning's news is of similar damage to Germany. Hitler has been extremely courteous to Petain in a discussion of peace terms or, as it's called, 'the reconstruction of Europe'. Hitler and Mussolini are reputed to be moving towards a pincer-drive on Egypt but I wouldn't like to bet on it. A map of Europe at the moment looks very depressing but a map of the world looks happier.

Wellington called Napoleon a blackguard. I'd like to hear his opinion of Hitler. The difference between Nap. and

Hitler, as I see it, is that Nap. was at least forwarding the aims of France whereas Hitler is only forwarding the aims of himself and his clique. Struck me with some force this morning, while shaving, that I *didn't know* why Hitler had gone to war unless for personal ambition.

8 November, Friday

Italy has now invaded Greece but it's an invasion that's gone wrong because by all reports Greece has penetrated Albania on her way to Italy. Also this country (Britain) has had time to land gear and troops in Greece all ready for a nice cosy campaign, that is to say, a soldiers' campaign. But as newspapers are so heavily censored as to make nonsense of them, as is the case also with broadcast-news, we are vague about what is happening anywhere except in the next village, and we aren't absolutely sure about that. But we can say, and thank God for it, that the bombing has slackened. No longer do guns boom at night, although we saw shell-bursts in the direction of Birmingham this morning. And although we had certain news of a man being machine-gunned while tending his dahlias in Kenton, we also hear of other suburbanites taking to their beds again and not being able to sleep for the sheer comfort of them.

As for us, we have had a thundering row with the land-lady, not unexpected. She was, after all, treating my wife as a sort of cook-general plus housekeeper, and me as a gardener. Luckily, the local Vicar, a man and family we much took to, has introduced us to another household of which the children have grown up and joined the armed forces, leaving ample room for the three of us. I fixed up terms (here, too, the implicit threat exists that with so large a house they are bound to have someone billeted on them, and we are as reasonable a family as can be expected) and meanwhile Jean has taken the baby to her mother's for three weeks holiday.

15 November, Sunday

Witnessed the bombing of Coventry, which must be forty or fifty miles cross-country. On my way to the Vicarage I saw all the flares, sky-twinklings of shell-bursts, and bomb-flashes of the old days. But the wind brought no sound of the bombardment. Now people say that, like the Great Fire, the bombing was ultimately not a bad thing because Coventry was also a planless, dirty, ugly city, whatever its history. Two hundred killed, eight hundred injured. I don't suppose any of the hundreds now rendered homeless thought it a planless, dirty, ugly city. This living in other people's houses has really impressed on me the tragedy of those rendered absolutely homeless and without the usual belongings.

This house began as a cottage but has been so enlarged that it now deserves the name of country house. All readers of *Punch* might be expected to own one like it, containing as it does Raphael prints, warming-pans, cigar-smoke, radio-sets like wardrobes, books, *Vogue* and a welcoming comfort. In the course of one evening I learned about Droitwich's underground river which is supposed to emerge somewhere in the Bristol Channel; about the curing of milk-fever in cows by emptying the patient's udder and refilling it with air from a bicycle-pump; about the frauds practised by young men and old women who instruct their brokers to buy for a rise and disappear when a fall occurs; about an RC baronet who fell in love with a C of E lady, married her in a registry office, and got fired from a sinecure as a result; about the conscientious objectors who live a hard life together in the cottage opposite with no women to wash for them and who bear no enthusiasm at all towards the Agri-cultural College which the tribunal has ordered them to attend; about the way a cousin made sufficient cloth out of one year's fleeces, when the family kept sheep, to provide all of them with coats and frocks for two years made out of the wool exactly as it came off the sheep's backs; about the Wizard of the Quantocks who relayed, in 1857, the first flash of lightning; about my landlady's grandfather who prophesied universal suffrage, but only for people over thirty, in a book called *Philadelphia* published about 1840; about Corbett, the Salt King, who purchased all the district's mineral rights from the Crown and died a millionaire; about the growth of the house we sat in; about Grafton House, former seat of the Earl of Shrewsbury, its dungeons, Priest's House, and dovecot; about the purchase of boracic powder for the tennis court, tennis tournaments on New Year's Day, past parties, and present emergencies.

Afterwards I wondered what had been different about that evening, and it was this, that we had sat through it all undisturbed by air-raids or a single explosion.

25 November, Monday

Unexpectedly I have got my family with me again, safely and with rejoicings on both sides. The telegram had given 3.30 p.m. on Saturday as the time of Jean's arrival. We had seen the Thursday and Friday bombings of Birmingham and on my way in by bus I saw the results: collapsed houses, gutted warehouses, wrecked streets, but now with two new features, the carrying of water from public mains, and the long queues of shopkeepers and others waiting for buses to take them away for the weekend. The queues had gone by 6 p.m. and an hour later the streets were deserted, black, wet, and empty. As it happened, there was no raid on Birmingham that night. The enemy has begun to localise its raids and devastate one town or area only. However, we weren't to know that, and the threat remained.

In New Street Station itself chaos and old night were reigning, also complete ignorance of what was happening. No trains were arriving from the south and I quickly discovered that no official lived who could tell me how long a passenger from Rugby would take to go to Stafford (for this was Jean's roundabout route) and come back to Birmingham. By 6 p.m. a small group of people like me had gathered in the lee of a tin-plate advertisement on the bridge crossing the lines peering out into the darkness for the first sign of an approaching train. My compassion was sufficiently roused to take a girl and young fellow, who were starving and seemed completely lost – they were waiting for the arrival of parents from Camden Town – across to the Midland Hotel and give them beef sandwiches and beer before returning to the pitchy hell of the station to meet a train that did not contain Jean. (Picture me whistling our recognition-phrase beneath the broken glass arch, trying to distinguish faces, and being accosted as 'David' or 'Tom', all the while waiting for the Bofors guns to start up and bombs to whistle down.) Then I took a WAAF to the Midland, similarly lost and starving. She was a fine strong girl who drove a lorry and trailer laden with gas-tubes for barrage-balloons between Runcorn and Malvern every other day. While there I telephoned the Cottage and heard that Jean had just arrived at Bromsgrove. So I took the WAAF part way to Moor Street Station and caught the last bus home. Gave all the food I had brought with me for Jean to an oboe player in the Bournemouth Municipal Orchestra: he now played the clarinet in the Royal Marines Band but his chief achievement had been to act as wireless operator in the *Exeter* in its engagement with the *Graf Spee*. Arrived back at the Cottage about 9.15 p.m.

Jean's story was characteristic of her. She had been turned out of the Stafford train at Tamworth and she was wondering what one normally does in Tamworth on a dark night when the Ticket Inspector said: 'That post office van is going to Birmingham. You can ask the driver and tell him Mr Taylor sent you.' Of course, the carrying of passengers in a mail van is as illegal as you can get but presently Jean

found herself sitting with the baby among bags of letters
and parcels in the rear of the van. She had then taken a train
to Bromsgrove and the daughter of the house had been good
enough to pick her up and take her to the Cottage. A guard
had left the push-chair on a platform in Birmingham but
otherwise all was well and it will be a long time before they
leave me again.

5 December

The Air Gunner son, Sinclair, came on leave last week. A
new type, at least to me. He had been a three pound four
ounce twin and was now only five foot eight tall but deep in
the chest and broad across the shoulders. A terrific dandy.
One would never dream that this prinked-up little man with
the slight lisp (perhaps affected), crinkly hair, and extended
elbow drinking tea, could spend twelve hours in the turret
of a Hampden bomber, mostly over Germany, either going
to or coming from Danzic. However, I have watched him
swallow three pints of beer, cap it with rum, and beat us all
at snooker. (But odd how beer-drinking is accepted as a sign
of virility.) His friend Greg, also an Air Gunner, told us
how they carry pigeons from local lofts in their bombers,
collected and delivered by van, strung up in a hamper, and
cooing away indifferent to speed or shrapnel, and released
only by day when stationary or sometimes while at sea, and
invariably, by official order, accompanying them in a 'bale
out' if the machine is shot down. The story of these birds,
owned, trained, and fed by private owners in back-garden
sheds, would make a curious postscript to the history of
air-warfare – the newest in man-made objects coupled with
natural things like birds.

Greg didn't bomb Danzic because he thought that snow
drifts were waves and thus lost his way. But he shot up
three supply-ships lying line-ahead near the Scheldt. Sinclair's usual job is to scout over the Atlantic at night on the

look-out for submarines coming up to breathe and re-charge batteries.

Boxing Day

Yesterday was a bit dismal in the absence of home, friends, and relations, with only a few cards and parcels sent to us. But we were in God's own heaven compared with many, as for instance Jones, the arthritic ex-Stock Exchange clerk who is living with his wife and two small children in freezing rooms with no cooking apparatus. Or the unknown untold thousands celebrating Christmas in shelters, the firemen, the soldiers, Stan Lock in Iceland, the conscientious objectors in farms, the lonely mothers and ruined shopkeepers, the city children living in farmhouses.

Forsan et haec olim meminisse juvabit (Perhaps some day we shall like to remember even these things: Virgil), who knows?

1941

I really ought to count my blessings because here I am housed in a comfortable office on sufficient pay while the AA gunners outside the Transmitting Station shiver behind sandbags. Might have been me. Jean is bored with no house to look after and is putting on weight, which is no bad thing. One has the impression of this countryside being scattered with disconsolate wives and children lodged in all manner of dwellings – farmhouses, Council houses, vicarages, and labourers' cottages – where formerly each had her own domain equipped with the latest labour-saving devices.

Fletcher's wife lives in the attics of a Victorian house down the lane otherwise occupied by a bustling family of youngsters and used by their father as an office. Jean walked down the lane the other afternoon with the idea of suggesting to Mrs Fletcher that they go for a walk together. However, Mrs Fletcher refused, and her manner suggested to Jean that she refused because Jean is the wife of a man (me) in a lower grade than that of her (Mrs Fletcher's) husband. If true, there's the true suburbanite for you.

A devastating raid on the city last Sunday night in which the Guildhall was burnt out. Some of the old churches went, too, as for instance St Laurence Jewry and St Bride's in Fleet Street, also Paternoster Row again. But St Paul's, the Bank, and the Mansion House still stand. A defeat, hurtful and savage. Roosevelt's Fireside Chat gratefully received – surely this is the first time he has openly and without reservation cited the Axis powers as the oppressors? Continuous mention of invasion. The general opinion is that Hitler will be forced to decide the war by open invasion of this country. Will it be in May, as it was in 1940 for France? We are supposed to have two million men trained and armed, which is refreshing news after the defeat of Dunkirk.

18 January

A snowstorm today following ten degrees of frost. I walked to work this morning, down the lane, over the footbridge, and round by the brook and the Flood, where I disturbed four wild duck rooting in the sedge. The powdery snow scurries ahead of you, and whispers over the roof of our shed-office. Drifts were curved round about the banks of the brook which flowed smooth and black beneath half-plastered tree-trunks. Yesterday a thick fog suddenly gave way to sun and we saw the trees in their rime like lacework against the blue sky, a perfect negative.

Not much news. Yesterday someone at the office said that he would never hereafter shake hands with a German or an Irishman. The pitiful Irish 'neutrality' affords no comfort to anyone, least of all to the Irish, many of whom have in any case joined the armed forces. It's the only member of the Commonwealth not to be in there with us, a typical Irish situation.

When we get back to our home all this will seem like a rather grey interlude but at the moment the future looks uncertain, a jumble of conjectures.

20 January

A howling blizzard has sprung up from the north-east bringing yet more snow. The wind catches the snow from the slopes and whirls it like spray over the fields into hedges and roads and gullies. On my walk to work I found among other marvels a mail-bag in the middle of a deep gully with a hat bobbing about ten yards in front of it, subsequently found to be the postman battling with a drift in a fog of powdery snow. Long icicles hang bent all shapes as they are prolonged. Intense cold in the office from draughts. A letter from the publishers to the effect that the Plymouth printers are without gas and water following last week's bombing, so that publication date of the spy story will be much delayed. Funny thing, why do I lose interest in a book as soon as I've written it and had it accepted?

2 *February*
Only personal news, that because our landlady wants the room for a married daughter we shall have to go. There's more to it than that, though. We surmise that the married daughter is a polite half-fiction. These two elderly people were growing tired of us, and who can blame them: Jean is at times furious when she is referred to her two rooms for the afternoon and as good as told to stay there, and who can blame *her*, either? So Jean and the infant will go to Newton Longville and occupy her parents' weekend cottage: what luxury, she says, to have the cottage, however small, to herself! As for me, I have found a lodging with an old couple in a Council house down the lane, and I shall visit Newton Longville as petrol allows, which appears to be every other weekend.

12 *February*
A marvellous speech and a long one by Churchill last Sunday in his appeal to the Americans. Reading it afterwards was stale beer after the oratory. His closing passage, 'Give us the tools and we will *finish* the job', was so intense that it kept a roomful of us silent for three minutes after he had gone. Oratory after the manner of Burke, unique today. The modulation, the cough or two, the bitter sarcasm and stronger invective – they won't sound at all when the war's over but they are still in my ears now. His genius is that

while he puts into magnificent words what we ourselves are thinking, he manages at the same time to inspire.

22 *February*

Complete and utter boredom. Eyes tired after nine hours at the office. Fletcher says he won't have private letters written in office-hours and kicked up a fuss when he found me writing openly about the insurance of my new motor-cycle. All those useful hours spent idling! Is it possible that some-day I may live my own free life? After such thoughts I look at the machine-gunners behind their sandbags, muffled up against the cold, and bless my comparative comfort. Only the countryside saves my sanity, the walk by the wild brook in the morning, the sooty-footed lambs I watch as I eat breakfast, the slope of a field and dull browny-blue of the hedgerows.

9 *March*

Visited Jean last weekend. The new bike, a 250 cc BSA, did the trip of seventy miles in only two and a half hours, which includes a stop for tea at a roadside café. It was lovely having ourselves together again, in our own home, even though that home be a makeshift one. Victoria was con-stantly round my legs, asking to play, and unhappy when I forsook her small affairs.

I sometimes wonder what turn the arts are going to take and whether or not to write a series of essays on their present values and tendencies before the war changes them. The chief problem in such a venture would be the lack of comparison for now we have no relative values of grimness, suffering, change, terror, and love. Who is to differentiate between the machine-gunner at his post and me in my office, bored to tears, longing for the freedom to write? All is absolute, with London besieged and Coventry demolished. Who is the genius who will show us the way out?

13 March

Last night a full yellow-red moon which brought to its peak the season's bombing raids. But no hard news comes to us either from papers or broadcasts. We just hear the bangs. My landlord, the jobbing gardener, was highly amused because, when we had both bolted out of doors, he by the back and I by the front, I suggested after a bang that made the doors rattle that he had only been taking his boots off. He was tickled to death by the joke and went next door to tell it again and reminded me of it next morning.

22 March

At six minutes past ten last night a Junkers 88, out of which the crew had parachuted some miles away, tore in flames past the Station masts, careered between Miss Maille's half-timbered Tudor house (in which incidentally two of our engineers are billeted) and its outhouses, tripped over the garden wall and burnt itself out. This morning the office-boy had his pockets full of machine-gun bullets, the rigging expert had found a pair of surgical scissors and five wireless sets (two for internal communication and three receivers) and when the rest of the office had had their pickings things like bomb-sights, bomb-racks, bomb-cases, altimeters, and odd bits of painted twisted metal were as common among the desks as bricks in a brickfield. One engineer says to another: 'Swap you my bomb-sight for your live bomb.' Over all this miscellany hung a faint cheesey smell which I noticed again in the lane beside the house. By lunch-time a belated guard had been placed on the wreckage. The house's escape from destruction was miraculous for the plane's wing-tip had actually scraped the ivy off its side.

5 April

In peace-time of course I should be off like a shot but it is impressed upon me that this job, however dull and frustrating, must be my contribution to the war-effort, that the department must work as a whole, like a machine, and that its purpose is as vital to the nation as any. This morning, by way of an underlining, comes a circular letter from Ernest Bevin, Minister of Labour, telling me as a Grade VI to stop where I am if I am engaged in Government work. And of course, at least in time of war, the BBC *is* Government.

15 April, Tuesday

This Easter – yesterday was Easter Monday – I have been at Newton Longville and as usual after leaving Jean I am still surrounded by the atmosphere of home, the familiar rug lying neatly across the bed, my own shoes beneath the radio, Jean in her apron paying for the milk, and Victoria trot-trotting round with a marble or a handbag.

One of the typists occupied my pillion as far as Stoney Stratford whence she took the bus for her home at Olney. Coventry has again been smashed and is under military surveillance. Birmingham is also difficult to get through according to Bird, whose home is at Shrewsbury. The young woman and I were stopped at Alcester for Identity Cards. Otherwise a smooth journey.

Jean's brother Jack was with us part of the time. Luckily Jean has her sister-in-law living near. Jack was already in RAF uniform and awaiting transfer to the photographic section. He told us a curious story of how his platoon (if that's the right word) were drilling on Blackpool promenade when he noticed a woman obviously in trouble among the breakers. Jack himself has many a cup and medal for swimming but of course he was not allowed to break ranks and go to the woman's assistance, and she drowned.

16 April

I notice in the hedgerows how quickly spring has pushed ahead this weekend. The sloe has come out with little balls of blossom, the lower twigs of the hawthorn are in leaf, and the martins have reappeared, twittering on telegraph wires. I should make a damned good Richard Jefferies were I not much more interested in people.

Retreats in North Africa and Greece are not compensated for by the routing of Italians in Abyssinia. The strategists fear – we all fear – that ultimately Egypt will be the next to fall.

4 May

A withdrawal from Greece, a threat to our oil-supply in Iraq, Plymouth pounded by raiders yet again. But I hear someone in the tobacconist's say philosophically: 'It only makes the war a bit longer.'

14 May

Journals may be extraordinary by what they omit and here I can't resist mentioning the flight to this country of Rudolf Hess, Deputy Fuehrer. The third man in the enemy's hierarchy has stolen away in a fighter-plane (which implies that he didn't have the petrol to get back) and landed according to reports on a Scottish croft and given himself up. The thing's a mystery – was he in danger of his life? Why come to Scotland? Why didn't he fly to a neutral country? Wild hopes spring up that he is bringing terms for peace but of course no terms whatever would be acceptable, short of total surrender.

3 June

Crete has been vacated and France itself is taking arms against us with the old, old cry of '*Nous sommes trahis!*' But President Roosevelt, who grows in stature every day, has thrown himself openly into the battle on our side. How the devil can I be expected to write appropriately of events like these! I can only write of things taking place under my nose, although I can't resist, as a storyteller, noting how George of the Hellenes crawled over sheep-paths and supped in a cave with a shepherd before being taken off by one of our own cruisers which is to carry him to Egypt.

Food scarce. I miss the vegetables most. Clothes are rationed from 1 June, not that rationing will worry Jean and me because the allowance is generous. Funny how the ordinary things of life are missed: when Jean lived here we took the bus into Worcester and there bought a small eiderdown for Victoria's cot, but because shops are now prohibited from using wrapping-paper or supplying bags we had to carry the eiderdown back home wrapped simply in string. No tobacco in the shops and cigarettes are a commodity for which one barters. No bitter at the New Inn tonight, I'm told. Queues at the sausage-shops but when you've got 'em the sausages are mostly breadcrumbs. For Victoria's second birthday Jean had raked together a feast of cake, chocolate, eggs, and custard, while in the morning we had ample bacon. I wonder what economies and fiddling Jean had made to accomplish it. As for razor-blades, one simply has to marry a shopkeeper's daughter before one can get hold of a new one.

8 June

Friday last I went with Gregg (Warden of the local Agricultural College) to visit a dilapidated farmhouse in scenery as bleak and wind-driven as any in Cornwall, where Gregg had set up a hostel of about thirty conscientious objectors. He says that they quarrel among themselves incessantly. When one of them saw that a gate had to be opened for Gregg's car and began to run, all the rest began to run, too, as though freshly released from mental homes. I was ashamed for my fellow-men. Yet Gregg told me that elsewhere he had 'planted' a hostel of men whom he judged to be men of principle rather than just idlers, and whose home was run smoothly in an atmosphere of austere efficiency and cleanliness. We came back to the college at 11.30 p.m., ate veal and ham pie and drank Oxo, a nice friendly party such as I knew often enough at Harrow.

My landlady, the old countrywoman, is tired of having me, won't give me a fire, grumbles about food, sulks, and privately (I am sure) criticises my every action. So I look for a room elsewhere. Sad that with home, wife, and baby I can't enjoy them but must hawk myself out to the most obliging householder I can find.

15 June, Sunday

The Barbers at Stoke Prior might quite easily take me in, at least for a spell. Nice people, very country, poultry farmers, who live in an old red-brick farmhouse on top of a hill with chicken cotes scattered round the slope of the hill. At the moment I am so hungry that I could happily live in a hovel provided the food were ample. Yesterday in Bletchley we paid sixpence for a cos lettuce, a shilling for two tomatoes, a penny each for spring onions. Sweets were tenpence a quarter, and neither cigarettes nor tobacco were obtainable. I don't mean to convey that we don't now have the funds to feed ourselves but that my present landlady keeps me short.

A week's holiday is in prospect. We shall pay London a visit. Jean looks really healthy and she is certainly happy because, although the cottage is not her home, at least she is her own mistress in it. She is growing fonder of the country whereas I, who dream of landscapes, now remember of it nothing but grasping shopkeepers, earth closets, and unhappy lodgings.

24 June

London is surprisingly unchanged: Oxford Street has been tidied up. The whole of Drage's is a gutted husk and whether ironically or not a notice has been put up, 'This

Site to Let'. Kensington with all its museums is apparently untouched. I came away with an impression of sleepy squares with cats yawning on windowsills, milk roundsmen brisk as ever, a clatter of typewriters within windows protected by chicken-wire, errand-boys' bicycles propped against the kerb. Went round to see Curtis Brown's, who will now act as my literary agents. Have a feeling that my visiting them has done me as much good as writing three novels – why, my 'Spy' story was made Crime Book Society choice for January and all I got for it was about forty quid. What a fool I've been.

Lumps like chestnuts in my throat when I left my small family safely home at Newton Longville. I told Jean that I didn't think I could bear much more of my present job but that Fletcher and the departmental head, not to mention Ernest Bevin, wouldn't let me go. She suggested that I didn't force the issue but waited for the right opportunity. She may be right because it's odd how, when you want something badly enough, chance puts it in your way.

A leisurely uneventful ride back to my billets, no preparation for its conclusion, which was a roused and storming landlady pouring out a stream of abuse the moment I appeared on the doorstep. She had found out all about me, she said, she had been through my things and found blacking things there which accounted for the smuts on the counterpane. And the filthy dressing-gown I had slept in! And the malice with which I had nipped out the buds of her orange-tree! God punished the wicked, my conscience would always be with me . . .

She sat beside the wireless receiver while Churchill was speaking, the volume full on and blaring over the hayfields, and when he had finished she swathed it round with a dust-sheet and tied string round it so that I shouldn't touch it. Then she fell to vituperation again, white with passion, so old and frail a woman, quite beside herself, her grievance only that I had blacked my shoes in my bedroom and her delusion that I had attacked her orange-plant. Told well, it would make a good story. I mean, it's too easy to say that she was a poor crazy old woman: what was in her to make her so? An old childhood grievance, some frustration of which she herself was perhaps unaware, a touch of the sun, revenge on me for a life merely of polishing, washing down, and peeling potatoes?

Luckily I have the Barbers to go to. As I left with my suitcases, Jack looked up from where he was digging, wanting to shake hands with me but not daring to because of his wife, and said: 'All the same, she's a good wife, she's a good wife.'

An anticlimax to relate now the startling news of Germany's invasion of Russia. The general verdict is that the more Russians kill the more Germans, and vice versa, the better. This happened last Sunday morning. Jean came out of the cottage to tell me as I was walking down the garden path, having just emptied the Elsan, and I said: 'Thank God, the pressure's off us.' Privately all I could think of was the precedent set by Napoleon, and look what a disaster *that* was! So far we have learned only that Brest Litovsk has fallen, that (great merciful God!) Hitler has promised Poland her independence in return for help, and that Russia has destroyed 300 tanks. We await *any* news – that Stalin has fled to Britain like Rudolf Hess, that the panzer divisions are in Nijni Novgorod, that Hitler has shot himself. The situation news-wise is that the papers and broadcasters can tell us pretty well what they like, since it doesn't concern the security of this country, but that they can't get hold of any news to tell.

I can't convey without writing an essay on the subject how calmly people are taking the news, since the collapse of empires is now an old story.

25 June

My room is a low-ceiling'd attic overlooking a wide view of neat fields and hedgerows fading into a far pearly distance of trees and hills. The hill on which the farm stands has a surprising steepness so that I seem to be able to lean out of the window and touch the two boys down the valley playing with what might be a tame rabbit behind a toy barn. The two transmitter masts rise out of a blue mist. The Malverns are their usual pictorial outline, sketched in roughly against the heat haze. I am not laying bets on how long I shall be allowed to stay here but so far I have been given all I want which, God knows, isn't much.

From the foregoing one can gather a hint of the universal euphoria following Germany's invasion of Russia. More smiles in the streets, the sense of strain lessened, Barber himself, my landlord, saying quite without thinking: 'Now we can get back to work,' which with him means poultry-farming. In fact, the euphoria is just a little dangerous because we still have armies abroad, which means sons and husbands, which so far have not been notoriously success-ful.

25 August

Just returned from a tramp with the .410 I bought for a quid in Newton Longville. No rabbits, but a riotous sunset, great clouds bursting out of the west in the blaze of a furnace. A long chat under a haystack with Wormington, the farmer, about asthma, rabbit-shooting, autumn sowing, earwigs, and compulsory ploughings. He says that the Bromsgrove medic told him that only the sufferer could cure asthma by finding out what gives it to him – tobacco or beer (both of them curses to me, even their aroma), cats, potatoes, sexual intercourse, or whatever. With him, it is cider.

A Churchill peroration last night, concluding with an Old Testament appeal to the enslaved nations of Europe to keep their heads high. Transpose the names and we might have been listening to Isaiah – 'The burden of Norway' etc. The Huns have reached Odessa, they threaten Leningrad and Kiev, but still the Russians maintain their ground and their obstinacy. The Finnish war was in our favour, after all. People say that if, by a twist of the wheel, Russia were to become our foe, they would go to prison rather than fight her, and it is true that many incline to communism as the way out. I ought to, myself, but from much reading of history I know very well that a dictator, or clique of dictators, must emerge from a communist state. The situation cries out for masterfulness, and gets it, from some conscienceless Caesar or other. So I remain apolitical, preferring the laughable variation of democracy in this country to turning Bolshevik.

28 October

Have just ridden back to the billet a big BSA combination that the Guv'nor bought on my behalf and vetted. Also I sold the old machine for £30 which is £4 more than I gave for it. Following the 'for sale' advertisement in the local paper I had a good many callers, mostly boys, but the bike went to a munitions worker of about forty who was scared stiff of it, knew nothing about motor-cycles, and gave me thirty notes of £1 each with great reluctance and suspicion only after I had handed over the bike, the log-book, and the receipt in the presence of witnesses.

Someone again asked what we were fighting *for* as distinct from *against*. No answer or argument in favour of this or that arose – not one at least that we could take seriously so as to bite on. This was over the lunch-table in the Station canteen. As for the *against* I suggested that Gibbon's description of the Alemanni in his *Decline and Fall of the Roman Empire* would give the answer. But then I am known to be bookish.

A circular from Broadcasting House asking for information about staff holding qualifications or merit not known to the Administration has prompted me to reply with a note of the titles of my published works. Haven't the faintest notion what the reaction will be, whether promotion to the post of Official Historian or instant dismissal for transgressing the infamous staff regulation which forbids private work except by permission.

15 November

Jean's birthday, and me separated from her by seventy-two miles. I phoned her last night and have sent her a wrap-over shawl, but the situation is a real heart-ache.

The new administrative chief at the office, who deputises while the boss-man is in London, must have been trained by the Gestapo. He makes little notes of things that go wrong, who's five minutes late, who is rude to whom, and who overstayed his leave. When he leaves his office he locks the door behind him and pockets the key, which in a close community like ours is tactless, to say the very least. This creature came up behind me this morning and with a pleasant chuckle, while pretending to read from a memo, said that the Administration took note of my literary work but in view of the urgency etc. etc. it recommended that I remain at my present post.

Shocks like this – humiliation – hurt – defeat – take a long time to sink in. Now I think, well, that settles it, I must leave this drudgery whatever the urgency, put the whole lot behind me and try to forget it. I am reminded that they didn't even have the courtesy to send *me* the memo, and then tell myself that I cannot afford the luxury of anger. Just go – get out of it.

8 December

Declaration of war by Japan upon the United States and

this country. I have just listened to the Premier explaining exactly how events shaped themselves (he didn't speak so robustly tonight, there were hesitations and throat-clearings) and a recording of Roosevelt's address to Congress. The Japs are like hornets in the Pacific, invading, torpedoing, bombing. We are told that there are 3,000 dead in Hawaii, for instance, following the completely unexpected attack on the American naval base there. No declaration of war, just an overwhelming raid by massed bombers. Also two landings in Malaya, and Guam and Wake Islands bombed. Out of all this appalling destruction comes an item that for some reason strikes me as farcical, the formal declaration of war by China on Japan, Germany, and Italy. Well, so long as we know where we stand! Thank God America must now be fully committed, for now we can't lose.

Difficult not to think that tomorrow I shall wake up and find it all a dream of some frightful continental film seen at the Academy in Oxford Street.

21 December

For the last four days I have been suffering from the foulest cough, cold, bronchitis, and asthma I ever remember. When specks of blood began to appear I struggled to the medic's in Bromsgrove and he made me feel a lot better at once by saying that the lungs were unharmed. Being poorly in an official billet is just too difficult.

31 December

Took a week of my annual holiday to visit Harrow with Jean and the infant. (She, by the way, has got as far as getting her words wrong e.g. 'Sing Song Eightpence', 'Tell story little of nothing', and 'Tell story New Lamps of Old'.) Lunched at the Strand Brasserie, still amazed at how little London, or that quarter of it, has changed despite the bombings, and afterwards visited Cecil Madden at the Criterion. He looked thin and nervous with overwork. When I told him about the proposed transfer to another department he again expressed an opinion that of all writers I was most to be envied, earning a living quiet enough to let me think and work in the evenings. Also, he said, a man with ideas – that is, of any originality – working for the Corporation has his brains picked and ends up exhausted and on the scrap-heap after twelve months.

It's a point of view Jean and I talked about on the way home without reaching any conclusion, except that we hate living apart.

1942

Three weeks ago my pharynx seized up and brought on chest trouble and sleeplessness. I felt as though I would cry if spoken to, which is no condition in which to pursue a living. Eventually I had to ask for three days sick-leave, which was grudgingly allowed. Came to Newton by bike along ice-covered rutted roads to find an empty cottage, for Jean and the baby were still at Harrow. However, they are coming by train. Met them at Bletchley and thereafter took to my bed, a couch in the little living-room, just about interested enough to read and listen to the radio. Frightening, really, to lose all one's volition even down to the use of one's legs.

Eventually, when recovered enough, I was sent by the local medic to University College Hospital in London because he suspected that the heart might be a bit out of position due to much coughing. Glad to find myself interested in other people again. Four different wretches with the genuine stuff of life in them also waiting for verdicts. One was a woman expecting her baby in February and going in for a second batch of X-rays to ascertain the nature of the trouble with her breathing: I remember the hollow, ringed eyes and the smile she forced to her lips when we found one another in dressing-gowns seated on the same bench. I wanted to whip her off to a South Sea island and feed her on sucking-pig and yams. The second was an old chap who complained that he fell down in the street due to a faulty Eustachian tube. The third and most tragic, a fellow in the last stages of TB – reported to have lived the last eighteen months in public shelters – could barely walk. The

doc said of him to a ring of grinning students: 'This man
has very little lung tissue remaining.' Me he described as a
characteristic asthmatic. I felt a complete fraud. I'm sorry,
I have forgotten the fourth but whoever it was, he or she
had existence, walked the earth, has the same value as any
of us – and I have forgotten him.

1 February

The X-ray revealed that all organs are sound. The lethargy
is purely nervous, due to working eight hours a day or more
in an army-hut at the far end of a frozen field, without
benefit of family, change, or worthwhile conversation. The
medic suggested that I change my job. So there it is, that's
how it's going to happen.

14 February

Still at the cottage, still without much energy, still surrounded by snow and ice. The doctor continues to give me
weeks off because I look tired and still have poor nights
because of nose and chest. Have ascertained at the local
Labour Exchange that I am not bound forever to the Corporation, that I am still on weekly notice basis, and that if I
become unemployed I shan't instantly be pushed into a
munitions-factory. The clerk was bored, having nothing to
do, and glad to talk over my problems. He said, yes, there
were still unemployed but these would never get another
job owing to illness, disability, liquor, or a criminal record.
Interesting that, to save electricity, many of the lamps in
the Exchange had been switched off.

News this morning of a stirring naval battle taking place
in the Channel between our planes and destroyers and the
Prinz Eugen, the *Scharnhorst*, and the *Gneisenau*, which
were trying to sneak out of Brest where they have been
pounded nightly by the RAF since ever I remember. (Cur-
rent joke: 'The Scharnhorst isn't looking so Gneisenau.')

But we are in a poor way, if not so desperate as this time last year: we are on the run again in Libya and at the backs of our minds is Singapore, still untaken. When at school I was taught that Singapore is impregnable and I thought then as I think now, What in heck is Great Britain doing in Singapore, anyway? All right, it's in a fine position to control the sea-lanes but I can't see that this off-shore European island (meaning ourselves) has any business there, Raffles or no Raffles.

15 March

A week of bronchitis, waking up gasping in the small hours and relieved only by ephedrin and amytol, taking Barber's hill in five stages and lying on my bed afterwards to recover – and all the time going to the office and nine hours of ledgers.

Came back about 26 February resolved to stay there no longer. Put up to it by Fletcher, the head called me in, in the first place I daresay to tick me off for my absences but in the end giving me leave to go. I don't know – men like him are no doubt shaping the world we live in but he doesn't know much about people – he alleged for instance that as a writer I must think engineers an inferior breed, and did I not think that radio engineering was an art. O God, O Montreal. The whole conversation made unreal by the squeaky voice left me by the pharynx. So that's it, then – when I remember walking round Newton Longville one frosty night praying and praying to be taken out of the present impossible situation, I can't help but believe that God intervened to help me. I must, however, stay on until the end of April.

29 April

Spent a weekend in town, chiefly to see if I can't get my lovely home back. As the Emergency Regulations stand at present, one can't give tenants notice to quit unless one can offer them alternative accommodation. Well, the tenants of 45 are nice enough people but I want my home back. By great good luck Curtis Brown's referred me to Hulton Press's *Picture Post* for a job. Saw Charles Fenby, Assistant Editor, who, on the strength of my books, offered me a chance to go out with a photographer and write up news-stories, at the same time emphasising that it was the pictures that really mattered, not the written matter.

Also saw Mr Tom Harrisson of Mass Observation but he could only offer £3 a week. (Mass Observation was a project begun in 1937 by Charles Madge and Tom Harrisson with the object of the 'anthropological' study of the British way of life. It carried on through and after the war collecting information from volunteer observers on every conceivable topic – football pools, drinking habits, the intimacies of marriage.)

As a final break, I sold the motor-bike and sidecar for £10 more than I gave for it. Last night the radio gave out that petrol for private motor-cycles was to cease on 1 November. Now, if that isn't good timing.

11 May

Was given my first assignment by *Picture Post* – and what an assignment! Even by their standards it was a peach, so much so that they didn't much want to give it to a novice hand. However, they did, and I was passed on to Pearson, the photographic chief, for briefing. Turned out that in days when our greatest threat is the submarine and merchantmen being sent to the bottom with a consequent loss of hands, private interests are maintaining a pool of Chinese seamen in Liverpool, absolutely contrary to national needs. At 11 p.m., at Euston Station I was meeting *Picture Post*'s photographer, Bert Hardy, and a Malayan interpreter, Ang Cheng Hoon. We stepped off the train at Lime Street

10 Chinese seamen in Liverpool. See entry for 11 May 1942. Photograph by Bert Hardy

11 The Kentish road-sweeper content on £2/16/– a week. See entry for 2 June 1942. Photograph by Bert Hardy

12 45 Pinner Park Avenue, North Harrow. Jean holding Victoria at the gate.

13 Monks of Belmont Abbey, Hereford, manning their fire engine. See entry for 23 June 1942

Station at 7 a.m., breakfasted at the Adelphi (untouched by bombs) and went to work. We found about 800 Chinese sailors living in doss-houses in Nelson Street, as it transpired – but how was I to know – a notorious quarter. They slept and ate and played cards on their bunks, which were of the rough-hewn three-tiered variety. But being Chinese they kept the place clean. Gentle people, not at all expressionless. Chinese sailors come cheaper than white and they were existing without pay on whatever the crimp passed on to them in rice. He was being paid so much per man to keep them on tap by the shipping companies.

Hardy went to great pains to get them to pose, huddled in their bunks, eating a bowl of rice ('He is thinking of his wife in Canton'), washing their clothes, and so on. We got a beauty of one seated on the windowsill. I questioned them as best I could through the interpreter, got their names, where they came from, what families they had, how long they had been in Nelson Street, and so on. That was all right so far as it went but I wasn't all that happy. It was too outlandish a story and I wasn't practised enough to be able to understand implications. Was I perhaps being fed a sailors' yarn? I confided my reservations to Hardy who suggested the Chinese Consul. Off we went to see him in a taxi and eventually I was allowed to interview him. A man of great dignity, not at all 'inscrutable' although careful what he said, who had an adviser on his right and an interpreter on his left, although he himself seemed to be able to speak good English. He confirmed the facts as I had ascertained them on the spot.

Then we made the mistake of going back to Nelson Street because Bert wanted some more pictures. The place was like a wasps' nest because the crimps, having got wind of our activities, had appeared with clubs and every intention of using them. As it happened we found ourselves at the back of an upstairs room with a mob of jostling Chinese between us and the door. Bert said: 'Never mind your head, that camera you're carrying cost two hundred quid,' and pushed his way to the door with me following. We made it all right and bounced into the waiting taxi with some relief. Why, racing down those wooden stairs, did my eye take in a quite irrelevant detail, a pair of worn pants hanging up to dry near a ventilator?

We returned by the 12.02 a.m. and I got off at Watford so as to have a bath and two-and-a-half hours sleep at Jean's mother's. Later in the day I presented my story at the office. Five hundred words had been asked for but I made it a thousand, on the principle that one can always cut but not always amplify. Fenby became excited – in fact, he stopped reading it halfway through and asked: 'Is this really true?' – and asked me to expand it to 1,500 words. I was shown into a small cabinet containing a typewriter on a desk, and was halfway through the rewrite when Fenby took me back into his office and showed me through into Tom Hopkinson's office. (He's the General Editor.) Here I was grilled about the truth of my statements for about twenty minutes. Lucky that I had had the audacity to visit the Chinese Consul! Then I went back to my cubby-hole to finish the 1,500 words. Fenby shook my hand before I left, saying that he would have to see solicitors on the subject of libel, as well as the Censor.

For this I am to receive £7 plus liberal expenses, and more if the story is published. Well, it made a change from ledgers in an army-hut in rural Worcestershire! Jean hugely enjoyed the situation. When asked in the course of the day where I was, she replied: 'Oh, he's interviewing some un-employed Chinese seamen in Liverpool,' to which whoever it was replied: 'Oh, yes?' and walked away feeling hurt.

(In fact, the story was never published because the Censor wouldn't pass it. His argument was that the enemy would get hold of it, reproduce its pictures, and scatter them over the Far East, saying: 'This is how the British treat their allied nationals.')

25 May, Whit Monday

Having heard at third, or possibly fourth, hand that a house similar to 45 was shortly to fall vacant, I went to see the agent and presently found myself slipping him two five-pound notes so that my tenants might have first refusal. Most reprehensible, I'm sure, but I wanted to see my wife's face when I told her that she could have her home back. And it worked! By going to see the tenants and taking steps to see that everything was ironed smooth I succeeded in getting them to accept it. Actually, they could not legally refuse but had I not been there they would undoubtedly have turned it down. The three of us went down to the Newton Longville cottage on Friday and spent most of the weekend packing and parcelling, ready for a neighbour to bring down on his brick-lorry. I brought back most of my papers while Jean came back with the ginger kitten in a shopping-basket. End of *that* chapter.

Jean's mother poorly with some illness that can't be diagnosed, or at least one that the medics are being mysterious about. Her skin has turned a golden brown and developed freckles, while she herself is so listless and (so unlike her) irritable. She took the bombing worse than most, and although we used to laugh at her complex preparations for spending the night in the Kodak shelters, there's no doubt that the continual strain has told on her. As I see it, this is how the strain is showing. Her husband, too, 'the Guv'nor', has been given twelve months at a desk job because his terrors during the bombing, although bravely masked, have given him shaky hands and a hesitation in his speech. Makes one wonder how many more so-called 'invisible' casualties are walking, or more likely lying, about.

A week ago I spent from 2 p.m. to 9 p.m. with the

Sunday Graphic in the News Room. Didn't like it a bit – too tough, all telephone and worry and no writing. Also, perhaps because I wasn't NUJ, I wasn't given any instruction in the mechanics of newspaper-making. I felt nervous and embarrassed and out of place. Still, if one is put on earth to experience, I have experienced a newspaper news-room and discovered that I am no use in it.

2 *June*

Another assignment for *Picture Post*. If the Liverpool venture was high drama, this one was pure comedy. Someone had discovered that roadsweepers in rural Kent were receiving only two pounds sixteen shillings a week (I could have told them something!) and someone else had described a graph of the wages of roadsweepers between Charing Cross and Brighton, high at both ends (about £5 a week) with a pronounced dip in the middle. So Hardy and I were despatched to find out how a representative roadsweeper in mid-Kent managed on the money, and to take pictures of this lonely man with his broom, thinking: 'How am I to buy a school-frock for my little girl on £2/16/- a week?' When we got there we found a well-kept cottage with a garden big enough to contain hens, a goat, two pigs, and vegetables enough for a platoon. Birket Foster stuff, with fruit trees, a big pile of logs, three little girls playing round a swing, and their apple-cheeked mother baking her own bread. Turned out that the roadsweeper looked upon his wages as a bonus rather than what he lived on – all the rest was barter such as I had met at Newton – 'Dig this lot over, Fred, and I'll let you have all the flour you want' kind of thing – and odd-jobbing, the occasional grave to dig, and his wife's wages as occasional help at the Colonel's. When we got back to the office the Picture Manager said: 'If anybody'll take my job I'll apply to be a roadsweeper in rural Kent.'

Victoria's third birthday on Sunday. Jean's Uncle Frank

turned up in Home Guard uniform with two stripes, also his family. A lovely day with children piling into the hammock while 'over there' a thousand bombers had spent a busy ninety minutes razing the ancient city of Cologne. Well, they asked for it.

7 June

Yesterday Jean and I and the infant visited 45 for the first time since it had been vacated and found its condition not so bad as we had feared, but more shabby than we liked. We were working until 11 p.m. lugging the heavy furniture downstairs and sorting it out, from where it had been stored in the back bedroom; carpets beaten, table assembled, light pendants hung, and so on. I couldn't wait to get out into the garden so, as the growing season is now well advanced, I planted thirty runner-beans, erected the poles for same, and dug over and fertilised the ground ready for planting tomatoes.

Jean said that it was her happiest day for years and, with recollections of those insufferable billets, I bet it was. She confessed that quite recently she had woken up with the cold horrors, imagining herself back at Mrs B.'s and shut in her rooms for the afternoon. Although by going into the country we were spared the latter end of the bombing and perhaps the nervous troubles her parents are suffering, we made a mutual promise not to leave our home again in any circumstances, unless forced out or bombed out. By God, no.

In the evening, although weary, she asked me what I should do for a living, whether I thought I could live by my pen, what hope there was of being able to put penury behind us. Didn't come to any firm conclusion (one seldom does, I notice) but it must have been three or four in the morning when we found ourselves wide awake, this problem still on our minds. I said words to the effect that, Look,

penury or not, I have been given my freedom when old
friends like Stuart, Bob Kieffer, and Stan Lock are in
uniform and separated from their wives and homes. Therefore it's up to me to find something worthwhile to do for the
country rather than interview roadsweepers in Kent. For
some reason I didn't confide to her my old haunting memory of the homeless in the Underground. Also a recollection
came back of my seeing in Willesden mothers with their
children milling round the entrance to a church, near which
two clerks were seated on stools at trestle-tables interviewing them. Included in the picture were two small boys, one
limping about on a crutch and the other bandaged round
the head. Homeless, I was told – the bombed-out whom the
Council is sorting out and trying to find shelter for; as for
the church, it had been loaned to the Council and was being
used as a Rest Centre. A sort of weary helplessness came
over me as I lay there at Jean's side, wondering why the hell
I couldn't be in there with them and help out?

Eventually we went downstairs and made tea. At four-
thirty it was already light and I walked round my garden,
mug in hand, thinking about nothing much. At least it was
my own garden I was walking in.

23 June

Third excursion for *Picture Post* a week ago, to a community of Benedictine monks at Belmont Abbey outside Hereford. Transpires that the Fire services are so organised that,
supposing Plymouth to be under attack (as it often has
been) the brigades from surrounding districts are called in
to help, and to fill the vacuum so created brigades as far
away as Bristol and Minehead either stand at the ready or
actually move inland. The monks have organised their own
fire-brigade which has been integrated with the system so
that, they, too, can be called upon to serve within a radius
of a few miles. So the cameraman took pictures of the

monks in their robes perched on their misereres during a service and then, ring-a-ding, racing out to don their fire-men's uniforms and helmets, lining-up, and climbing aboard their fire-engine.

Brother John acted as spokesman. Nice chaps, sturdy, very clean-looking, with open faces. Two or three were obviously 'religious'; withdrawn and inward-looking, pale-faced, who never met our eyes or, if they did, seeming not to see us. A lesson read while the evening meal – fish-pie and fresh fruit – was in progress at the long refectory-tables. Lovely surroundings, cattle lowing in lush meadows, wil-lows, bee-hives, enough vegetables in the vegetable-garden to feed a regiment, flower-borders, herb-garden etc. I was told that the establishment was self-supporting. As for the purpose of it all, I learned that the abbey provides a channel to God that is always open, that such channels must always exist throughout the world, that the abbey was in effect a prayer-factory, an idea first encountered in Aldous Hux-ley's *Grey Eminence* (a biography of Père Joseph, a Capuchin friar and diplomat in Richelieu's France). All the same, during the office of vespers to which I was invited I felt uncomfortable and inept, not to say excluded. Slept the night in a 'cell' so-called that was rather more comfortable than other cells I had slept in as a bachelor, if without the tennis-cups.

Not much of a 'story' for the paper but it occurred to me that no novel I could remember had a monastery and monks as a background, unless it was a French one, and that if I could get hold of something that told me exactly what were a monastery's organisation, routine, 'offices' (meaning ser-vices) etc. I might have a go at a serious-type thriller. On the way home, I became very excited by the idea even though I am well into the book on the early days of broad-casting.

Physique not up to such assignments – I was in bed two

days after this one. Jean said that for my health's sake I
ought to see if I couldn't get a worthwhile job ('worthwhile'
meaning a contribution towards winning the war) locally.
When I told her at last my reactions to the plight of the
homeless she suggested that I go and see the local Council.

Meanwhile golden days of freedom make me feel a bit
guilty.

19 July, 1 a.m.

The monastery thriller will have to wait because Curtis
Brown have sold the rights in the broadcasting book to a
new firm of publishers on the strength of the first four
chapters and a resumé of the rest. Let's hope I can finish it
in the next twelve months.

We have finished painting downstairs, while wondering
how many others will come back to *their* homes, sooner or
later, and find them in need of paint. On the Wednesday
Robert Kieffer paid us a social call and stayed to take off his
khaki jacket and wash down the walls with sugar-soap.
Owing to flat feet he's in the Pay Corps. Told us a horrid
story of how, while looking out of the windows of his place
of work in Alexandria, he saw an Arab shambling down the
street suddenly pounce on a kitten, screw off its head, stuff
the body under his bernous, and idly toss the head away.

Jean's mother suffers from an extraordinary lassitude in
addition to a greenish-brown tinge of skin. The medics
suspect an infection (or possibly TB) of the endocrine
glands. She is bent like a query-mark and when she must
rise hobbles like an old, old woman. And when I remember
what she was before the bombings! I hope Hitler's pleased.

This is written in a Fire-watch period, shared by all the
neighbours, in which I am duty-bound to stay awake.
Three shifts a night, and at 3 a.m. I shall take the log-book
to the Fields at 44, having received it from Mr Gower at 1
a.m. One gets an awful sinking feeling when one gets no

response to one's knock for it means that the occupier is asleep, duty or no duty. It takes me two days to get back my physical well-being after such a session. Heaven knows what I should have been like in the army, still more so the navy.

16 September

Called for another look at the War Artists' Exhibition in the National Gallery and think Sir Muirhead Bone's picture of the minelayers the noblest. The pose of the oil-skins over the shoulders was reminiscent of one of Rubens's Allegories in which the same bow-shape – left arm, shoulders, right arm – is made by the fleshy woman. The most striking pictures were the Eric Kennington portraits. Thence to the Royal Academy of which a half was given up to the *Express* exhibition of war photographs. The *Express* has been given a free hand – God knows what the RAs are thinking – a carpeted salon for killed VCs with palms and soft music, and the central hall given up to a display of the Atlantic Charter and its ideals, resounding with marches and anthems. Overdone. Well, I always had a soft spot for the *Express* because it published my first schoolboy article, written in longhand. All the same, this was pure cinema in which a mighty Wurlitzer wouldn't have been out of place.

The Fire Brigades' artists drew quite a different class of crowd, bigger for one thing, even though the Nat.Gal.'s pictures are superior. People are frightened by the Nat.Gal. and don't know whether or not to take their hats off. The chief reason, however, was that here were hung scenes of disasters that the public themselves remembered and had perhaps participated in. Also, everybody wanted to express their admiration for the Fire Brigades which, throughout the blitz, never faltered. They hadn't been *in* the front line, they *were* the front line.

8 November

Last week we were given the news of the routing of Rommel's forces in North Africa. The end of a legend, apart from anything else, because he was supposed to be invincible. The man who routed him is said to be of the traditional Bible-in-one-hand-sword-in-the-other school, a tremendous egotist. Well, so was Nelson! Yesterday the landing of 'tens of tens of thousands' of American troops in Algiers and Morocco – they say it's the 'first battle in the war of liberation'. Funny, I thought we had been fighting the war of liberation for some time now, all by ourselves. A train of surmises follows, talked over at street corners and in pubs, chiefly whether or not this is the so-called Second Front or whether yet another invasion, of Europe, must follow or take place separately, perhaps across the Channel.

16 November

Now that Jean's mother has returned from hospital she has been installed in our back room, the very same that sheltered us during the bombing. Indeed, we look upon her as though she herself were a victim of shrapnel or flying glass. Talk of 'being without her' and 'executors' brings tears to Jean's eyes, as to her father's. He is so filled with gratitude to us for taking her in and nursing her that he cannot see me doing anything but wants to better it for me. He sees me polishing my shoes and offers to go up home for some special Probert's oil. He found me putting up an extra coat-rack and presently I found his tin of rawlplugs in my hands. He is getting draft-proofing for the front room (draught-proofing – it's 7 p.m. and I am tired) and arranging for us to have a telephone.

My chief concern of course is Jean.

A week ago I was interviewed for a job at the Council offices at Stanmore with the Rehousing and Billeting Department. It is this department that looks after the bombed-out and London evacuees, so it seems likely that I shall get the job I've been after since leaving the BBC. Oddly enough, the tragedy of Mamma urges me to take the job even though the pay won't be much and, the way the war's going, we aren't likely to get many more mass air-raids. One of the specialists I saw about the asthma, at the Marylebone place, described me as emotionally immature. If this means I have an instant bottomless compassion for the deprived and the oppressed then I don't in the least mind the description. This compassion is nothing to boast about because I was born with it, i.e. I didn't have to earn it by some experience of keen suffering. An RC priest once described me as 'having grace' and one supposes that this mysterious phrase is another way to put it.

6 December

I have completed the Broadcasting book, had it checked by sundry experts, including my brother Alan who objects to the 'pack of cards' technique, and handed it in. A long book, my first serious one, of which I have high hopes. By chance the *Radio Times* mentioned that nobody had yet written a history of radio (although Leonard Mosley wrote a light book on the subject) so I wrote to them telling them what was happening and in their reply they ask for a copy of the book when published so that they can mention it in their columns.

So I have no misgivings about taking a job again, even though the wage is only £4/8/- a week. But no travelling expenses, except for wear and tear on my old push-bike, and I can come home for lunch. Jean can't disguise her pleasure. A change from Droitwich! There, I should still be living at the Barber's, separated from Jean by seventy miles, and deeply unhappy. Here I am in my own home and growing fat on it. Even the little cat contributes to my content – it slept on my shoulder as I sat reading a book about shipwrecks, my feet on the mantelpiece. Even as I sit here typing, Jean is trying a Christmas frock on Victoria, up for the first time after being found with mumps. Whereas, in a Forces' Air-mail letter written four weeks ago, Stuart Littler describes what it's like travelling across the Deccan, India, in a compartment crowded with other soldiers, in stifling heat, at thirty-five miles an hour.

1943

On Boxing Night at ten to seven in the evening Mamma woke from a drowse that had kept her unconscious on and off for a couple of days and asked for her milk. The Guv'nor was at hand to comfort her and stepped out of the room to boil it. When he returned he found that in turning over to ease her cramped legs she had died. I heard him call out – I was washing up at the time – and in the hall he said: 'I think she's gone.' I went inside and felt the pulse – a queer sensation to feel the wrist still warm but with no tick in it. A tear had rolled onto her nose. Jean astonished me by her resource and strength.

The office is going very happily – plenty of freedom, little worry, fresh faces, and home for dinner. The work entails finding lodgings for nurses employed at the Orthopaedic Hospital at the top of Stanmore Hill. It is said to be chiefly occupied with mending broken airmen. Worthwhile work, therefore, but surprising the resistance one meets in householders. I knock at the front doors of well-to-do households and am met with the widest variety of women and excuses. The most common response is: 'Oh, you're from the Council. No, thank you', and a door shut in my face. As one might expect, it's the poorer people who have most sympathy, but there again it's the poorer people who have most children and therefore all their rooms occupied. Still, so far I have managed by guile and much smooth talk to get three nurses accommodated.

This experience bears out what Ted P. was saying one evening last week (a solicitor's managing clerk, a friend from pre-war days) that if I am to write novels I should write about the lives of dockers and lorry-drivers rather than about professional people like doctors and radio engineers. He's got a point there. Dockers and lorry-drivers are more humorous, sympathetic to others, and (come down to it) experienced in the business of living. Professions tend to weave mysteries round themselves and thus separate themselves from humanity. Money separates, too.

21 February

Tomorrow I must start the story of the monks, provisionally called 'Bluegown'. I don't remember loyalty in a man, sufficiently strong for him to conceal that the man he is loyal to is a homicidal maniac, ever having been used in a thriller before. So it's in 'Bluegown'. The publisher's list with *All Space My Playground* came this morning. Out in March.

A good many people think that the war will be over this year. The Russians have recently retaken Rostov-on-Don and Kharkov. Our own forces are in Tripoli and pushing on to Tunis. It's very naughty of them, but the office men – all old soldiers of the last war – are secretly delighted that the Americans have suffered a reverse in Tunisia. Clowes said: 'That'll teach the buggers.' The 67-year-old Churchill, just returned from Casablanca, Turkey, Cyprus, and Tripoli, is now getting over a bad cold. We have had a three-day Commons debate on the Beveridge Report (on the feasibility of a National Health Service) and it has officially been declared possible provided that the country can find the money after the war.

21 March

Jean is just leaning over the table showing me the clothes she is sending to the villagers at Newton Longville. Although I must agree that the dark green velvet dress is really too old to keep, I can't help feeling sorry for I remember when she made it, in the dark days when I was with H. in Bishopsgate.

This morning and last night I took part in a full-scale Civil Defence exercise, operating from the Honeypot Lane Rest Centre. How my mother would have loved to see these modern welfare centres, fully equipped with beds, or rather bunks, mattresses, blankets, mugs, cutlery – every conceivable article and convenience, including a clinical-looking canteen, ready at an hour's notice to admit refugees. Honeypot was intended to be a clinic and library but has never been used as such. Instead it was organised by the Home Office, acting through the UDC, to take in what had been foreseen as a flood of refugees pouring up the Edgware Road, after the French pattern. The London refugees never happened, not in any great number, that is, and the Rest Centre was therefore used as a temporary shelter for the Urban District's own bombed-out.

We have come a long way since milkmen were ordered to tie their horses' heads to trees as soon as the Alert sounded, and all traffic to stop.

I watched the WVS take charge of the 'rendered homeless' as they appeared, one with pretend-measles, one only in her nightgown and rendered helpless by a fit of the giggles, and another with pneumonia who 'died' in the night. In the morning (Sunday) I reported at 8.30 a.m. and made 27 calls at addresses given to me by the WVS, secured 40 billets, and filled 13 of them with Unaccompanied Children. Pearswood Gardens I found to be Out of Bounds due to an unexploded bomb and that after I had placed three families in it. When I asked a Warden about the disposal of the supposed UXB he replied: 'It's no use asking me, old cock, I've been killed.'

After it was over and pronounced a qualified success we all went home to Sunday lunch. Unless I am particularly dumb I don't see the point of the exercise since Hitler is much too busy on his withdrawing battlefronts to bother about us again. Or is there something I don't know?

A revisiting of people the Department rehoused a year or two back brings me stories of suffering now a little stale. I see oil-paintings on the wall pitted with shrapnel and flying glass, a woman's face pock-marked with tiny dimples from flying glass, a girl of 25 with a plate in her back and a false arm, always on the verge of tears, a woman in receipt of alimony (when she can get it) from a husband who ran away with a German woman now interned, and the bitter and poor and very often ungrateful. I have to confess that the people from West Ham and Whitechapel make their own slums wherever they go. The Council may have rehoused them in a pretty semi-detached with mahogany doors and parquet flooring, but (in the case I saw) an old gas-cooker has been used to plug a hole in the hedge, the pavement outside is littered with rubbish, and one of the tiled hearths and its surround has been bodily removed and, one presumes, sold. Mrs Busby, with a family of five grubby infants, has created a permanent stink that gave me a headache in ten minutes. Mrs Sherratt, living rent-free in a self-contained flat with refrigerator, curses the Council, the war, me, and her 'posh' neighbours. But then her old man is in North Africa and her eldest boy was killed in the blitz. Naturally much friction arises between such rehoused families and their neighbours, who were (most of them) living here before the war started.

Can't resist putting down the story of the gravedigger who, when his wife was taken away and put in Shenley (the local Mental Home), took up with another woman and had three children by her. But then, at the outbreak of war, he was asked by Shenley to take his wife back because the institution was anxious to unburden itself as much as possible. And he did so, with the result that when his cottage was rendered unsafe by the Hatch End bombs, the Council

14 Demolition of the surface shelter outside No 45, after the war

15 A watercolour by George of the garden at No 45, painted about 1946

16 George at the end of the war

found one wife living upstairs and the other downstairs. And this was how they were rehoused, for a Home Office ruling is that under no circumstances must morals be questioned by a local Authority: as they are found, so they must be rehoused. When I interviewed him, primarily to find out whether he could contribute more towards his subsidised rent, he was suffering from recurrent malaria, contracted in Australia's Northern Territory. He had also worked in the Chicago stockyards and in the Canadian backwoods, logging.

What was it Ted suggested, that the lives of dockers and lorry-drivers are the more interesting? Let's include those of gravediggers.

30 March

Two notable items of news, the first is the taking by the 8th Army of Rommel's Mareth Line in Tunisia, the second is Corky's confirmation that we can expect a fourth member of the family to arrive about the end of October.

5 April

Corky was wrong. We are both dreadfully disappointed.

16 May

This morning I was pricking out marrow and cucumber seedlings and heard the cuckoo call at the same time as the church bells were ringing for the African victory. Even Marlborough, even Wellington, had an army still at large in the country he was fighting in. Here is an 'invincible' foe cleared out of a continent. The times are so grey and life so pared down to mere existence that we needed those church bells.

18 May

My birthday. Last night much entertaining talk by Ted.

When I said that I really didn't know why Germany had gone to war again unless it was for revenge, Ted seemed to rise to it. He said that the Germans were fighting for a myth of which Hitler was the symbol. He must have been storing up ideas on the subject because he went on: 'We are all of us longing to believe in something. We *must* believe. We believe in Robin Hood when there was no such figure, and we believe in King Arthur when he was only a captain of mercenaries. Lawyers have taken advantage of this longing to create an unassailable empire of precedents, doctors a ditto of credulity, and priests a ditto of superstition.' Jean said mockingly: 'Oh, yes, and what may we believe in that we can be sure is true?' and he replied: 'In yourself, my girl, and your own promptings.' At some time he said: 'The last people you want to believe in are experts with vested interests. I mean, look at Estate Agents who have the nerve to use the motto: "Experto Crede". Whoever believed in an Estate Agent and didn't get robbed?' His usual cackling laugh. He said: 'The Jerries must have been shaken to their roots because Rommel's hoofing it back to where he came from. The invincible Rommel! Another myth exploded.'

Still shabby but a lot tidier than when Jean and I had found him on his bike in North Harrow, unshaven, stinking of tobacco, without a tie, and rotten teeth. A disastrous second marriage, he told us, to an Austrian who had only wanted a British passport. Jean had made him visit us and he had gone on visiting us, each time looking a bit more civilised. The foregoing is only a condensation of the talk. After Droitwich, what marvellous conversation! It's like bread to a starving man.

5 June

We met Stan Lock, who is on Survivors' Leave. His new command struck some unknown underwater obstruction, which may have been ice, and went down. A destroyer

picked up all but four of the crew. All his personal belongings went down, including Will Durrant's *History of Phi-
losophy* that I had lent him. Before he had gone off he had
said: 'George, I want something lengthy that I can get my
teeth into', and I had lent him the Will Durrant book as well
as a large tome of the *World's Best Love Stories*. Difficult to
reconcile my tennis partner and the producer of *Ruddigore*
with icy seas and a sinking ship. I asked him if it were true
that the captain was always the last to leave a sinking ship
and he said: 'Not on your Nelly', but he didn't enlarge.
Same foxy smile as we burst out laughing. If I had been one
of his crew I should have absolute faith in him.

I learn that 'Dink' Sugden wasn't so lucky. At school, we
passed messages to each other in class as we fixed up a
camping holiday at Penmaenrhos, North Wales. It was
arranged that we should meet outside the school at eight-
thirty, and when I cycled the three or four miles to Wol-
stanton to find out why he hadn't turned up he came to the
back door towelling his head and mumbling that he had
overslept. I didn't forgive him until Chester was behind us.
He had always wanted to be a wireless operator, and he had
succeeded. His Lancaster didn't return. The same with
poor, charming Derek, Jean's cousin, whom we chiefly
remember sitting on the roof of the downstairs kitchen, at
our Cricklewood flat, counting the trains. Jess (his mother)
still hasn't given up hope. She says: 'What must he have
thought as the plane went down. I really can't bear to think
of it.'

19 June

The Deputy Clerk put me onto a Book Scrutiny Committee, otherwise composed of Councillors and clergymen. It's
part of a salvage drive in which the whole of the Urban
District was asked to put out what books it could spare,
these then being sent forward as reading-matter for the

armed forces. With mixed feelings I came across a copy of my own *Spy Who Died in Bed*. This was in an abandoned mansion at Hatch End that has been requisitioned but found to be beyond repair and restoration.

18 July

The publishers report that 2,000 copies of my broadcasting book, *All Space My Playground*, were ordered before publication. Now it's out and the 'Broadcasters' in the *Radio Times* say it's the best book yet about broadcasting. Mac, formerly one of my Droitwich bosses (not the one who fired me) sent me his views on it: he says that I have over-idealised the engineers, their dedication, professionalism etc. At least it gives the lie to his colleague who came out with the childish notion that as a writer I must look down on them.

14 August

The counter at the office has been rushed by the over-crowded of Wealdstone and Queensbury. They have read that *all* the requisitioned houses are to be released and *all* the overcrowding relieved. The truth is that we must keep a dwindling percentage for our two priorities, the blitzed and the war-workers. The reply these unhappy people make is that the blitz was over long ago, or hadn't we heard. My heart chiefly goes out to the young marrieds living with in-laws: one learns in this business that it's a law of nature that two women cannot share one kitchen. However, I now understand the satisfaction an official behind a counter feels when he says, No! I understand it but don't employ it – with me, it becomes a challenge in the variety of smooth talk I can put across.

21 August

The other evening (to condense a four-hour stretch) Ted

asked: 'All right, what are we fighting for?' He didn't really want an answer, having stored up his own since our last session, but I said: 'We couldn't stand Gauleiters, especially the Scots. I wouldn't put it past the Irish to welcome a Gauleiter in place of the English, though. If ever they get one, God help him.' Ted said: 'Come on now, I asked what are we fighting *for* not against,' and Jean told him: 'My little Arab upstairs.'

We had two other visitors, Joe, the crippled ex-navigator, and Susie, his wife. Joe said: 'The number of times I've heard that question asked', and Susie suggested: 'Freedom.'

Loose replies like that always 'fetch' Ted who began a long prepared soap-box address on the theme of 'What bloody freedom?' when Jean said softly: 'Now, Ted.'

His regard for her isn't far short of adoration for it was she who had given him back his self-respect. He stopped short at once and asked me: 'All right, George, you tell us what we are in it for.'

I couldn't reply. Nor can I now. I remembered that first job in the Hanley insurance office with the shadow of the '£235,000,000 In Reserve' lettering (it may have been £189,000,000 – who cares when it comes to sums of that amount) thrown across the clerks' backs as they earned their £80 or £100 a year (of those sums I am sure). Also Walter Hutchinson, the publisher, bringing out my Spy book as a paper-back with the words '77th thousand' (itself a lie) on the cover while refusing to pay me more than my initial £40. Also those Chinese seamen in Liverpool, the victims of unbelievable treachery and avarice on the part of certain shipping companies.

All I could say was: 'They'd either march me into a gas-chamber or send me to Poland to dig roads, in any case separate me from Jean.'

It was all talk, really: none of us, least of all an individualist like Ted, could have borne an invasion by Germans or anyone else. Ultimately, beyond Jean, were my Stafford-shire forebears, who go back to the fifteenth century. It's a true thing, this Englishness.

Marvellous how Jean manages to provide sandwiches and cocoa while putting her 'fat little Arab' to bed, all in ten minutes.

3 September

On this, the fourth anniversary of the outbreak of war, here are two indications of how it is affecting society.

I was sent to Golders Green on the track of a defaulting rent-payer, one of our rehoused. His name appears on the books as Leamington. At the address given me by the Food Office (nobody can go into hiding these days) he was living as Mr Ford together with a Mrs Ford. Furnished rooms. The landlady said that he had been absent for about a fortnight and that he had reappeared with a beard and broken finger-nails. By the face she made I understood prison, particularly as he had subsequently had letters re-addressed to him from Brixton. I met Mrs Ford, who is really Miss Ford, a plump blonde girl four years older than Leamington. By coincidence she had been a typist em-ployed by my friend, the Welfare Officer at Napier's at Borehamwood. She (the Welfare Officer) told me that Miss Ford had been fired for ' "carrying-on" – with anyone she took a fancy to, a labourer, a clerk in the cashier's office, and now Ford.' Leamington himself has a legal wife in whom pregnancy has brought on TB. She now lies at Redhill Hospital and he was given his term at Brixton for failing to maintain her. Between his wife and Miss Ford there had been another woman who had come and gone from our requisitioned flat in Stonegrove.

None of this would have arisen in pre-war days when neither of them, Ford or Leamington, would have dared to risk losing a well-found job.

The other indication found its way into our own home when Jean stood at Pinner in the same bus-queue as Mrs Flaxton, who lives with her pretty daughter Sharon down the road. Out of neighbourliness Jean brought her home to tea. A remark about nerves and ill-health brought out the information that two years ago Mr Flaxton, a corporal with the AA, handed her a wrong letter betraying the traditional 'other woman'. Eighteen months ago he told her that he could no longer live with her, she must realise that she was getting on (she's thirty-three) and that he could, and did, pick up any girl he fancied simply by leaning across in a cinema and asking for a light. Later he went on (out of cussedness, I should think) to describe his latest girl's underwear. Six days of his last leave he spent with his mother and in the short space of five hours spent at home he knocked Sharon spinning and called his wife a hag. Last year she had tried to do away with herself. She is ashamed, she says, to show anyone the inside of her house because she can take no pride in it. The garden, too, has been allowed to run wild. (In this she's not unique: the number of gardens I come across that had once been their owners' pride and joy and are now only dreams in the minds of men in Italy or on the high seas.) She paid her husband's CO a visit but was told only that her case was one of hundreds like hers. She is still devoted to him, certain that he will come back. His behaviour, she said, was quite out of character, formerly he had been withdrawn and shy.

8 September

From the 6 o'clock news we learned that Italy had surrendered. Half an hour earlier the departmental head had called me into his office and asked me to familiarise myself with the duties of his deputy, who has been notified that he is to receive a commission in the REs. Didn't want the job. For one thing it's all office-work, and for another I have already been aware of a hint or two of resentment by the permanent staff towards us temporaries. We are only suffered as a necessary inconvenience that will go the minute the war's over – Local Government politics are as hot inside as out. So we compromised. I am to take on some of the work but not to be given the title. My wage at least has gone up to £6/5/- a week. The deputy described the practical tests the army had put him to before granting him a commission. The first was to get over a wide ditch without getting his feet wet. All the help he had was from a rope and a stout cudgel. However, he had watched from a window how a candidate preceding him had tied the cudgel to one end of the rope and thrown it into the branches of a tree in the hope that it would catch, which in the deputy's case it had. The other test was to manoeuvre a 'wardrobe' round a series of concrete corners.

19 October

A big gap, but then nothing much has changed. I still cycle out to try to find billets for nurses, but the field is pretty well exhausted. Also billets for workers at Napier's, rather easier because the pay is better. Predictably, one of the permanent staff has gone in to complain of my taking over some of the deputy's work. I have finished the 'Bluegown' thriller which is now called *The Staffordshire Assassins* – the latter word I fell in love with after reading Freya Stark's *Valley of the Assassins* – all those 'a's' – what euphony, what poetry! Now the book has to be checked, with particular reference to the religious ceremonials and 'offices'. After that Jean will type it. Then it has to be rechecked. Then it has to be sold.

Two bombs fell last night in Hall's fields, behind Pinner Park School. Alerts are increasing in number. Milk scarce. Meanwhile a substantial public shelter has been built outside our front gate so that we can troop into it when the evening sneak raiders arrive. When the Alert goes we get things ready, when the guns go off we bring Victoria down to sleep behind the settee, although occasionally we take ourselves and our bundles into the surface shelter. Victoria is growing aware of the war and mentioned the word for the first time last week. Also she asked if that aeroplane in the sky were a German. Jean attempts the impossible task of trying to explain what's happening but the child will never know the alarms we've suffered.

17 November

Following the huge Russian drive, now almost into Poland, bets were being laid in the office that the European war will be over by Christmas. But now the date is June of next year ('44). Threats of our invading Europe – bombings of Norway – an insurrection in Denmark. The first years of peace are going to be difficult. I know for myself that once I have left this job I shall never again seek employment. And how many hundreds like me, weary of uniform, are saying the same!

Oranges are back again in the shops. The biggest crop of tomatoes this year that I've ever had. The green and pink ones alone – i.e. those not ripened – filled a barrow. We couldn't have got this far without the garden to give us green stuff.

18 December

On Monday the 6th I came home with a slight cough and sat down in the fireside chair. Two hours later I was so weak and wretched that I couldn't undo my buttons and Jean had to help me and lift me upstairs. This was the onset of the prevalent 'flu that has decimated the office. Jean and Victoria, thank God, have so far escaped.

Particularly Jean! She is booked at the Nursing Home at the bottom of the road for about 25 July next. We aren't afraid that the fifth year of the war will have any permanent effect upon the baby. We are glad, and that's all there is to it. Besides, babies and nursing mothers are given preferential treatment in all sorts of ways: the babies are given concentrated orange-juice, drawn by coupon from the Food Office in Wealdstone, and the pregnant don't have to stand in queues but are automatically passed to the head for their fish, oranges, etc.

The tree is set up in the front window and half-decorated with pre-war gew-gaws. Balloons are blown up and lanterns hung. But we are none of us feeling particularly riotous.

1944

New Year's Day

Two days ago I was told that *The Staffordshire Assassins* had been accepted. So that's all right. Also I was told that *All Space My Playground* was the firm's best-seller, as it is mine. More immediately, confirmation came through from the Ministry of Health that I was to be promoted to Senior Billeting Officer, which carries another pound a week, back-dated to 1 October.

Meanwhile the victories are piling up – great advances by the Russians who may now be thought to threaten Germany itself. Also the seventh mass raid on Berlin last night, and increasing rumours of the opening of the so-called Second Front, the invasion direct of occupied territory. The rumours are given foundation by a talk over the counter with a one-time member of the tennis-club who knew me well enough to confide that he had witnessed a rolling of tanks down the road towards Southampton, and from the air had seen assemblies of all manner of craft in all manner of creeks and inlets along the south coast. He himself was an aircraft fitter-inspector who, as he said, 'went everywhere'. The information was murmured over the counter at the end furthest away from the others. All right, such information must be kept under one's hat in case it falls into unfriendly hands but I can't help thinking that, if it were broadcast, what a wave of enthusiasm it would rouse in the poor suffering public – what a boost to morale.

Still weak on the legs from the 'flu even though I have been back at the office for a week.

20 February

Friday night's raid left a trail of ruin in most of London's boroughs and lost Harrow its charmed security. The sirens went about ten to one in the morning. We were undecided whether or not to get up for we are now having the first bitter weather of the whole winter, but a tremendous up-roar of barrage-guns drove us downstairs and into our one-time shelter of the pantry. A crash on the roof and a breaking of tiles about 1.05 a.m. was later found to be caused by a lump of shrapnel, as we guess the bottom casing of a shell. At 1.10 a.m. four bombs fell near us in College Road and College Hill Road, Harrow Weald, near Leslie Henson's house (Leslie Henson, the pop-eyed star of light comedy). At the time Victoria was singing 'George Porgie'; only some minutes later she confessed that she didn't like the bumps. Like ten thousand other kids, she must think that 'war' and bumps in the night are the usual state of affairs.

All the following day and for six hours this morning I was getting my first experience as Information Officer, having requisitioned the front room of a shattered Nursing Home which I had turned into an office.

(Here I must explain that following raids earlier in the war the Home Office had learned that nothing reassures the bombed more than the simple word 'Information' printed on a card and stuck as near as possible to the site of the disaster. What had been a private catastrophe was turned by this word into a matter of public concern. In an office thus requisitioned lists were compiled, principally gathered by the WVS, of the people who had been gathered in each of the affected houses before the bombs fell, and of those who could be traced afterwards. Some inevitably were never traced or identified. It was then my job, again as laid down by the Home Office, to acquaint the nearest blood relations of the deceased or seriously injured and in hospital, or to see that this was done. First and foremost I had the job of

helping the injured or homeless to begin life again by direct-
ing them to the nearest Rest Centre, handing out certifi-
cates which could be used as evidence to railway booking-
clerks that the holder had been made homeless by enemy
action and should be given a free ticket, and in some cases
obtaining money for them from the Public Assistance Department. Also present was a WVS lady in charge of their
store of second-hand clothes. Apart from the loss of life in
his family, a man might present himself in his pyjamas,
having lost all he possessed; in wartime, when papers such as
identity-cards and ration-cards were necessary for
existence, a good deal of grief might follow, and replace-
ments for these, too, must be found.

It should be remembered that these Women's Voluntary
Service ladies were housewives. They would give their
children breakfast and see them to school, or get their
husbands to undertake these duties, before turning up on
site in their neat, serviceable uniforms to undertake any job
their Commandant required. Sometimes this job entailed
cleaning a house through, where for instance a housewife
had a lot of children, because the first thing any bomb did
to houses on the perimeter was bring the soot down the
chimneys. I don't know what these ladies do nowadays,
when they are 'Royal', i.e. WRVS, but they certainly have a
tradition to live up to. Not everyone could get on with their
Commandants, who were once described by a friend of
mine as the 'put-the-wounded-over-there' type, but as my
mother had been of the same type I was practised in jollying
them along.

I must also add, for better understanding of events when
the V1s and V2s began to arrive, that of course I wasn't the
only one to man such emergency offices. The department
consisted of the head, myself and a colleague whom I will
call Gates, two women welfare workers, a retired builder
and an assistant who managed the requisitioned houses,

while back in the office proper a secretary/typist might always be found. Overall direction of the Council services was in the hands of the Controller, who in our case was the Clerk to the Council, a quiet man of unshakable nerve. Harrow Urban District, now absorbed into Greater London, was at that time the largest such district in the country.)

To my surprise I found myself able to do the job, practical for the first time in my life. After all, this was the work I had wanted since the war began. A stream of the slightly injured, the bereaved, the indignant, the homeless, the bewildered passed through the office. Let's hope to God I was able to satisfy if not comfort them. Bitter cold, alleviated by tea from a mobile canteen opposite, with the clink-clink of tilers employed by the Surveyor's Department and shouts of rescue squads coming through the open windows. The Surveyor's men are the first on the job, after the rescue squads, the fire-brigade, and the police, restoring what houses they could and giving first-aid to others by throwing large tarpaulins over broken roofs. The speed with which the operation proceeds is astonishing, I suppose in the first place because the 1940 raids, relatively slight though they were in our District, have perfected method. Ultimately, I imagine that the workmen feel as I do, although many are Irish: as men not in the armed forces they can at last do something to help defeat the enemy. Note: thick-soled shoes are essential for this job (a) because of broken glass, and (b) because they keep the cold out.

Now every night we prepare ourselves and our immediate valuables (including marriage certificate, identity-cards and ration-books!) for a quick transfer to the Surface Shelter in the road.

23 February

The siren goes about 2 a.m. or at almost any time. It always wakes me. I rouse Jean, we leap into our outdoor things, and while Jean grabs a bagful of valuables and papers, I come down with Victoria in my arms, as often as not fast asleep, and we hurry out to the reinforced Shelter so conveniently placed near the front gate. This has already been opened by the Fire Guard – normally it's kept locked against lovers, and small boys taken short – our paraffin-stove is lighted, and we settle down with our neighbours in the three-tier bunks. Other Fire Guards drift in – one night while somnolent we were all roused by the most appalling crash which turned out to have been a visiting Fire Guard's steel helmet dropping onto the concrete floor – while outside the night becomes noisy with bangs, crackles, and rumbles rolling round the heavens. The clouds light up with gun-flashes, flares, and path-finding cascades of light-globules nicknamed candelabras. Sometimes a green or dusky red ball comes floating through the clouds. Fires are started on the horizon while behind it the clouds glow a dusky red. A plane zooms overhead. Shrapnel cracks on the rooftops. And gradually the noise dies down and the lights go out. Meanwhile I have been praying that the bombs will fall outside the Urban District because we have our hands full. It makes one think of inner suburbs such as St John's Wood, Islington, or Dalston. How are *those* local authorities coping?

Last night a spectacular local fire was started on Harrow Hill and – God, what an outrage! – the school tuck-shop was gutted. The noise was tremendous. We woke to learn that a high explosive had destroyed a bungalow in Rayners Lane, while two UXBs (unexploded bombs) have put 106 people out of their homes into the Corbin's Lane Rest Centre. The counter this morning is crowded with applicants for Morrison shelters. These are iron-plated cages with lattice sides, about nine feet by five by four, that one erects inside one's home, preferably in the recess provided by the chimney-breast. But sometimes I see them outside, clear of buildings, why I don't know, because they are intended to be furnished with mattress and pillows and slept in.

Also the wretched blitzed from the London inner boroughs come to implore us for help in finding a roof for them. We can't because we have only a small and dwindling stock of requisitioned houses for the use of our own bombed. A fine balance has to be made between immediate requirements and what houses we have to keep in reserve for the future. Naturally the situation lends itself to abuse and complaint, which our two women welfare workers bear as best they can. Actually, I deceived one of them by telling one customer, who convinced me that she had three children, a husband in the services, and had walked from the Elephant, to come back next day and say she had originally lived in Northolt, part of which comes under our care. Naughty of me. The rule is that one must never allow oneself to become personally involved.

This is written in the Fire Guards' Room at Harrow Weald Lodge, knowing that tonight the circus will start up again and that I shan't be at home to lend a hand. (And it did. All the Luftwaffe seemed to be overhead.)

11 March

A lull in the raids, thankfully received. I wonder if Victoria will remember how her father nightly carried her, half asleep, into the roadway Shelter, and bore her back again when the All Clear sounded? Jean stands it well, being filled with an inner determination that nothing shall go wrong with her. The baby is due in four months.

29 May

Part of history is that fact that Enid from No 41, Christine from the Crescent, and Audrey also from the Crescent – all three being handsome and desirable young girls ranging from ages 17 to 20 – have developed patches on their lungs. If this isn't a direct corollary of war I have never heard a bomb drop.

Of greater national importance is that we are presently under the shadow of the so-called 'Second Front' (actually, this will be the third or fourth front) by which is meant the invasion from these islands of the continent. Although dead secret, much seeps through, how the Americans have been pouring tanks, guns, and equipment into this country, how the respective armies have been given different objectives – the Yanks here, the Canadians there, the British somewhere else, and how the invasion will be preceded both by a massive air-bombardment and an attack by air-borne *gliders*. I find this incredible, even though gliders have been employed by the Germans. Much of it is rumour but at least it has given the office old soldiers a great deal to talk about.

A grim kind of exaltation is in full flood. I daresay the actual sailings will not be dramatic because dispersed over days and over the north European coastline.

7 *June*

The sailings were dramatic but when news of them came they did not appear to be so. While cycling through the quiet streets yesterday – only prams and buses, bicycles and tradesmen's vans (very old, with their place-names half-obliterated, relic of the 1940 anti-invasion precautions) – I found it difficult to believe that not two hundred miles away blood and thunder is in progress. Even then, having a stuffy head-cold which keeps my head ringing, I shall never be able to put the events of 6 June 1944, into their proper perspective. Such is the force of a subjective viewpoint!

Jean heard the 8 a.m. news of warnings to the French, and of German reports of landings, but it wasn't until I was interviewing a woman in Buckingham Road, Edgware, about 10.40 a.m. that I learned that the invasion was fact, and going on at that moment. Since then we have heard a soldier's speech from Eisenhower and a rousing speech from Montgomery, and a speech from His Majesty made touching by his stammer. Also a number of eye-witnesses have given descriptions of progress with more understatement and less hooey than those voice-reporters usually give to a cricket-match. Perhaps they have realised that for the first and only time in their lives these are events that don't call for exaggeration. Difficult in this quiet room, with Victoria asleep like a cherub on a cloud in the next room, with Egglestone going by, as he usually does, riding two bicycles, with the neighbours strolling by to walk their dogs – to conceive of bloody beaches and a flaming night only across the Channel, where in 1938 the Kieffers were taking their summer holiday.

Formations of single and twin-engined fighter-bombers (Mustangs, Lightnings, and Thunderbolts) fly low enough for us to see their blue and white invasion stripes, winding slowly north-west at this hour (twilight) to their fields and hangars in Wiltshire and East Anglia. Like starlings coming home to roost before another day's foragings. Sometimes they throw out a couple of brilliant recognition lights. Everyone comes out to watch them and wonder how soon they will be off again, among the armadas which now each morning fly out one or perhaps two miles above our rooftops, southwards.

12 June

That word 'invasion' only touches the surface of the mind. We don't really *think* about it, I suppose because it's been on our lips these last eighteen months – 'When is the Second Front taking place?' and so on. We won't ever understand what must have been the long-distance planning, the decisions of detail that had to be made, the final assembling, co-ordination of forces, the order to go. And in man-made things details are always going wrong, failing, or being lost. And in a huge enterprise like this! Even to describe it, supposing I were omniscient, wouldn't convey a hundredth part. Words are so limited, and movies not much better.

Well, whatever's going on over there, my sympathies as usual are with the unknown, the forgotten, the buried alive, the mutilated and disfigured who won't ever appear except as a name in a paper, or perhaps as a photograph on a piano in a town in Indiana or Alberta or Yorkshire, 'Bugles calling for them in sad shires', anonymously.

One thing about a soldier's death is that it doesn't entail the paper-work that follows on that of a civilian. Following the latest spate of bombing we even had a young fellow call in the site-office asking half-humorously how he could replace his matriculation certificate and letter of reference as to character from an employer now in France. Interesting case in itself as he was a soldier on compassionate leave from the Pay Corps who saw his first bit of action when a bomb fell on a house across the road and deafened him.

Other side-effects of bombs are the stripping of leaves from wayside trees, the deaths by blast of sparrows, chaffinches etc, and the awful things that happen to cats and dogs. We had a man complain that thirty of his forty-odd small birds in a backyard aviary had been killed by blast, half a mile or so away from where the bomb had landed.

18 June, Sunday

The latest development to affect our lives is the 'Bumble Bomb', which is a pilotless aeroplane carrying a cargo of high explosive let loose on the continent and pointed in our direction in the hope that it will land where it will do most harm. Our first intimation of this menace was a noise like a

motor-boat fifty feet above our heads first thing last Thursday morning, the 15th. I sprang out of bed to find out what
on earth it was but it had passed out of sight by the time I
had reached the window. I said: 'A plane out of control, I
should think', but Jean, sitting up in bed and leaning on one
arm, said after awhile: 'Georgie, you don't think it's *something new*, do you?' Since then we have heard two or three
of the damned things, in the distance. Amos had heard
what they really were from somewhere. Sparing of comment, as usual, he said: 'See you in the Shelter, then.'
However, we haven't yet taken to the Surface Shelter because Jean is now pretty heavy and uncomfortable. She
sleeps downstairs behind the 1940 barricades while I sleep
with Victoria in the big bed upstairs in case she grows
frightened, which she was last night. Heaven knows what
permanent effect all these bumps in the night and other
strange noises are going to have on her!

Our neighbour on the other side, Woodstreet, who is a
railway policeman at Euston, had seen three last night, and
gave an impression of their flying over in droves – or should
the word be flocks – at quarter-hour intervals. They land
anywhere within the Greater London area but more especially in south London, just as though south London had
not already had enough damage inflicted on it. This is
indiscriminate bombing at its most blatant, its object being
I imagine to cause the civilian population to demand an end
to the war. Its effect is quite the opposite for it rouses
anger.

Most annoying is the official statement that we were
taking their measure, having known about them for months
– why, in the next sentence they say that they don't even
know whether or not they are radio-controlled! As usual
they are toning down a real threat though it has many times
been demonstrated that the best course is to tell the public
the worst and ask them to face it – at least they know *what*

to face. Only Churchill and Woolton know the secret of imparting confidence.

25 June, Sunday

About 9 p.m. last Sunday when walking up Parkfield Avenue, having just seen Mrs Moody onto her train at the station, I heard a now-familiar buzzing and looked up in time to see one of the bumbles lurch and fall, a Spitfire overhead watching it. A loud Whoomph! and up sprang a great billow of red dust.

I ran home and then cycled off to the site with Gillie Amos, she in black dancing-slippers. We found devastation off Gayton Road, an area of well-to-do houses near the middle of Harrow. Hundreds of cyclists were being held back by the police, sightseers later to be much condemned. But then this wasn't a dog-fight or a fire, it was something that affected all their lives. I ought to say 'our lives' because Gillie and I were among them.

Guessing that the boss would need me, I hurried home, and was duly picked up by him half an hour later. We (or at least I, for the boss was busy with overall liaison with the other services) picked an office in Gerrard Road and at once began the process of collecting information about casualties and damage, posting up notices as to where the different kinds of help could be obtained, suggesting what was needed of the invaluable WVS team – this was Sunday evening but there they were, all turned out in their green uniforms – and generally taking over from the Incident Officer.

My office had been a good-class home. (Surprising how, in the face of such disaster, the owners were more than willing to let me use it and have the public walk in and out!) The oak-panelling facing the window was like sandpaper with tiny splinters of glass. Brush your hand against it accidentally and you needed bandaging. Even the remaining armchair could not be used for the same reason. Elsewhere I had seen a face or two that had got in the way of such splinters.

I stayed on the job until 5.30 a.m. when a car was ordered to take me home. By that time the line of customers had thinned, and the telephone company had installed a field-telephone. There might be no customers at all but I still had to get in touch with the Personnel Departments of the army, the air-force, and the navy to inform them that so-and-so's parents were in hospital, or whatever. I slept four hours and was back on the site at 3 p.m., staying, absolutely drugged with fatigue, until 10 p.m. On the Tuesday, Gates took some of the work. On Wednesday about 5.30 a.m., when Jean had just made tea after emerging from the outside Shelter, another one came down the other side of the Kodak playing-fields, shaking us a little and busting our backdoor lock with the last wave of blast.

The same process began all over again but with less fatigue. For one thing the houses there are more widely spaced and not so big, but still – six deaths and about fifteen seriously injured. Also I was learning how to conserve energy, while tracing next-of-kin, getting a message sent to a wife through the police, seeing the Surveyor's foreman to suggest that, because of the human problems contained in a certain house, it might be given priority. I found in myself the same capacity as at the Harrow Weald incident some months back to suggest and improvise and assume responsibility. I say this because I had been a clerk for so many years and it was nice to find authority in my makeup. I foresee that if this menace continues – if the invading armies don't overrun the launching-sites – I shall have to watch that I don't become inured.

About now, however, guessing that we must have more to arrive, I got into the habit of having a small case handy packed with forms, notices, writing-paper, pencils, drawing-pins, and so on. Also a pointed stick on which to pin the 'Information' card. I took to noting down useful addresses and phone-numbers such as those of the police Super. when he was at home, of factory Welfare Officers and of useful people to contact in the services, as well as the more obvious ones such as Public Assistance and railway welfare services.

Surprising how *localised* these explosions are. In the usual way any one of them would attract throngs of sight-seers. Now that everyone knows what they are caused by and what they look like they keep away, thankful I suppose that they have escaped. I cycle on my way to one, most often first thing in the morning, and find people going about their business as though loud explosions in the neigh-bourhood were the rule. Then at the end of a street one finds great activity, brisk and orderly, and somewhere a crater in which muddied men from the gas, electricity, and water companies are busy, the usual chaff, cigarettes being smoked (except of course when there's a supposed gas-leak!), men in steel helmets gathering in knots to decide the best course, all surrounded by rubble, small semi-detacheds with their roofs blown off, and further away tiles still slithering off roofs, odd bits of furniture in front gardens, householders in all sorts of garb, many of them with cuts, sweeping up, rescuing papers and valuables, gossiping ('Well, I'd only just put the kettle on, you know what Frank is, when –'), or in my Information office shivering as they patiently wait their turn. Overall the faint cheesey smell I first noticed in Worcestershire.

Since the Parkside Way 'incident' (old words take on new meanings these days) we have had no more bombs and very few alerts. Perhaps the enemy is at last feeling the effects of the RAF's attacks on the launching-ramps along the Pas de Calais. Jean and Victoria are sleeping in the bottom bunk of the Surface Shelter, all the same, while I doss down in the back room, the French windows barricaded with books and meshed over with chicken-wire taken from the carrot-bed. Jean is determined to remain calm and she succeeds even though I have noticed sturdy WVS women flinch and tremble as the bumps resound in the distance. There is a frightening quality in these bumbles not associated with the piloted bombers. Ted P. suggests that women in particular find their non-human element more terrifying than the bomb itself. One recognises the buzz as one lies awake and immediately begins to tense-up – I have felt my muscles brace themselves – for the engine to cut out and the thing to drop. And when it does, one waits for the bump, and when that's come, one wonders whether or not it has landed in Harrow. I mean I do. But then noises at night have always been deceptive.

At Gayton Road about six hundred houses were seriously affected – ceilings down, doors off, roofs ripped off, apart from the house and four flats which were so completely destroyed as to be simply non-existent. Only four killed and twenty-one in hospital. At Parkside Way six were killed and only three in hospital, with perhaps five hundred houses affected of which about sixty were made uninhabitable. My first intimation of the Parkside Way incident, after cycling through Headstone Park, was seeing a boy of 10 in a dressing-gown crossing the street with a jug of water in his hand drawn from a street stand-pipe.

The dawn armadas continue, especially on clear days. Long processions of four-engined bombers in formations of thirty-four, a cross-stitch against the blue.

Writing all this is perfectly useless except that it serves as an outlet for a mind oppressed with too many vivid images.

2 *July*

The menace has been renewed. Last night I was so heavy with fatigue, eyes aching and brain numbed, that another bomb in Harrow would have found me wanting. But the bomb did not come, although two resounding crashes in the night weren't two miles distant. Took a Luminal and slept from 9.15 p.m. to 7.30 this morning, apart from a short spell about 3 a.m. when a crash roused me and planes buzzed. This morning I took the Guv'nor to see Parkside Way and Station Road, cleared up the latter and brought the papers back with me – ultimately to go to the Home Office, for statistical purposes, I imagine. Even the Guv-'nor was impressed. As an engineer he doesn't have much understanding of writers, and otherwise he has seen me only as a poor devil of a clerk, so I was glad to show him that I was good for something else.

We have now had five doodle-bugs in all, viz: those at Gerrard Road, Parkside Way, Shaftesbury Avenue, Kenton Gardens, and Station Road. On the average, in our outer suburb of rows of semi-detacheds, each bomb kills five people, throws about twenty into hospital (some with appalling injuries) and puts thirty families out of their homes. One of those tragi-farcical incidents took place at Kenton Gardens, which is better class property than most. A WAAF called Mary had been seen by her neighbour coming home on leave to one of the shattered houses. This was in the evening. In the morning nothing could be found of her. The Controller happened to call in so I told him: 'We have this young woman Jessie from the same house, apparently a sister. She was at the pub in the main road last night and is now staying with relatives at Wembley. Both parents killed.' The Controller h'mmed a bit, then went outside – this whole incident was made memorable by the floods of rain that incessantly came down – and ordered the Heavy Rescue squad to turn over all that remained of the wrecked house, rafters, bricks, doors, what was left of the windows, in an effort to recover the missing Mary. Mean-while I had got onto Mary's HQ at Bristol to obtain confirmation that she was indeed on leave, which she was. In the middle of it all Jessie happened to drop in for a certificate to say that she had indeed been bombed out of her home. While writing it, I asked her: 'We're a bit worried. Do you know where your sister is?' 'Sister?' she said, 'I've got no sister. I'm an only child.' I said: 'Then who's the missing Mary? Is she with you?' Laughter on her part. (I ought to have mentioned that she was quite a piece, strong-looking, bursting with health in spite of being tossed out into the garden by the bomb, and dressed in a nice two-piece.) 'I'm Mary,' she said. 'I'm called Mary in the WAAF and Jessie at home.'

I ought to have known. I myself am called George by all and sundry but something else by my family. The Heavy Rescue squad were the only ones not to be amused. Jessie-Mary had needed the certificate as evidence to her Quartermaster that she had lost her uniform by enemy action.

On our way this morning, the Guv'nor and I were buzzed by one of the infernal machines but it droned on towards Watford and I haven't heard where it fell. Normal life is quite literally paralysed. Housewives run to the shops and run back to hang round their homes and duck at almost any noise overhead. Such children as go to school are said (by Amos) to spend their time in the Shelters, in which lessons of a sort have been organised. At the office, which is representative of most, I imagine, an unspoken trepidation is always present. Our ears are forever cocked for *that* drone. And this is an outer suburb! What can be the effect of one of 'em landing on those tenement flats in Fournier Street, Spitalfields, where I used to collect rents? Or on the Mansion House, or on Buck. Palace itself?

We are told, without anything being certain, that some 75 per cent of the things are shot down in open country or brought down by fighters which fly alongside, get a wing-tip under the machine's wing-tip, and flip it over. Sounds a trifle hazardous to me – a placebo administered by Whitehall doctors. We are also told that no serious damage has been done although Bush House, the Regent Palace Hotel, and one of the Charing Cross bridges are all said to have suffered. But then I have little information I can believe about London town, and none is given by press or radio. We are all 'southern England' to them. Rumours abound, springing up from nowhere, that we are next to experience shells powered by rockets. Rumours also abound that we are about to make a separate invasion of the Pas de Calais to quash the nuisances.

Victoria sleeps within two yards of me in a bed she has chosen for herself inside the fireside kerb, while Jean still goes to the immovable Surface Shelter. (I have seen these structures standing untouched, except for a single slab pushed out of place, within twenty feet of an explosion.) Jean is now within three weeks of her time. She appears to be unperturbable, her only complaint that she's been turned out of her comfortable bed. The Guv'nor is now sleeping here. At this moment, while I sit writing in the little bedroom that I have turned into a study, my ears are cocked for the ominous buzz so that I can call them all into our barricaded parlour. This has the additional strength of the double wall dividing us from the Woodstreets, and of the chimney-breast – almost always, if anything is left, it's the right-angle made by the chimney-breast and the dividing wall.

5 July

Now there's a diversion. The department head called me into his office this morning. Apparently the Heavy Rescue squad over in our corner of Edgware is dissatisfied because they don't have separate lockers in which to put their things and secure them. They were in fact on the point of striking, and were holding a meeting that evening at the Honeypot

Lane Rest Centre, and would I go to speak to them on behalf of the Council. I was thunderstruck. Me? Why me? Why our department? Weren't they the Surveyor's responsibility? And how are Rescue Squads made up – of whom, when they are obviously big rugged men whom the army would have welcomed. As for replies to the first questions (my boss said) the Controller himself had nominated our department for the honour and had mentioned my name. As for the last question, the men in question were mostly Irishmen. I felt utterly incompetent to address a crowd of dissatisfied Irishmen even when I learned that (a) a Trade Union official was to be present, and (b) lockers with padlocks were due to arrive any day now from the Office of Works.

It was a challenge, and I have never been known to refuse one yet. I reflected during the day that many of the Heavy Rescue had seen me on site more than once and that therefore I could be said to be one of them – that is, in the struggle with them. Also I reflected that if I could interview a crowd of out-of-work, dissatisfied Chinese seamen, a crowd of dissatisfied Irish workmen would be child's play.

So I went, push-biking through Wealdstone, along Lockett Road, through Stanmore, and into Honeypot Lane itself when I might have been digging my garden back home. A large number of men, about fifty, only a few of whom I knew by sight but to those few I was at pains to give a wave of the hand or smile. Shook hands with the Union man. New experience, entirely. All except me were 'brothers' for some reason. Ritual. I spoke first, very briefly. Scared as I was and facing a crowd of orderly quiet men prepared to listen, I said: 'You may think that I am just another Council man. I am not. My name is such-and-such and I live at that address in North Harrow. I have a little girl of four and my wife is a fortnight off having a second child. For me, this is a wartime job. Many of you have seen me on site, doing the paper-work. In fact, I am a writer of books, one or two of them thrillers that you yourselves may have read. I took this job because the services wouldn't have me on account of my being a chronic asthmatic. My country is under attack from a new kind of bombardment, and if there are any Irishmen present, they will have realised by now that their country, too, is in danger. My country is short of manpower, as you may have noticed, and that is why I am here tonight because there's nobody else. I forgot to say that recently I have been made a Senior Billeting Officer, which means that my wage is now six pounds five a week, less deductions. (This made 'em think for most of them were knocking up twice as much.) I have only one question to put to you: You aren't thinking of going on strike because of a shortage of lockers, are you?'

With that I sat down, to everyone's surprise. The Union man looked at me before rising. He said: 'Well, has anyone any questions before I tell you what's being done about the lockers? Whatever Mr Beardmore may have told you about his private life, he's here representing the Council.' Dead silence until a blessed Midlands voice spoke up from the back rows: 'Ar, they can ask 'im if he's found Mary yet.'

Universal laughter except from me. The story must have gone the rounds. The Chairman explained that lockers were being taken from the WAAF stores and would be with us in a week's time, and meanwhile would they be satisfied to use the ones at the nearest Rest Centre. There was no further mention of a strike.

When I phoned the boss at his home to tell him I noticed that my hands were trembling. As well as his voice I could hear a background of soft feminine chatter, and the unworthy suspicion was borne in upon me that he had given me the job because he had funked doing it himself.

9 July

No further bumbles have landed in the Urban District although a good many have crossed it on their way north. Also no day passes but we hear tragic 'whoomphs' to the south, meaning in Wembley, Kenton, and Neasden.

This morning I saw off my first party of evacuees. (As though we hadn't got enough to do! And essentially such heartbreaking work.) Only thirteen this time, for Harrow is only permitted to send the homeless, not for instance the children, mothers, and mothers-to-be who are being despatched north by the unhappy southern suburbs. A harrowing scene on the station, quite different from the laughing and chattering queues of kids sent away in 1940 and 1941. This is the first group I have actually organised and personally despatched. Five or six of them I recognised from bomb-sites. They go to Chesterfield in Derbyshire. Never get personally involved.

30 July

Anthea Frances born Friday morning 1.30 a.m., the 28th. This was in the Nursing Home at the bottom of the road. When I walked in first thing I said to Jean: 'I was going to bring you the sunrise for a present but I had to leave it behind.' Still a bit washed-out but nothing like so badly as when the first came, Jean said: 'That's nothing. Look what I've got for you.' Two fly-bombs had landed in the night, one in Rowlands Avenue and the other in Old Redding, neither of them very far away. Jean had made the nurses put the cot on the far side of the bed from the sliding plate-glass door that kept her in a perpetual state of fear. But all was well. I told her that the third that morning had landed by coincidence in a field – not, thank God, in the crowded Silver Estate – in the same neighbourhood as the other two. Blast from it had flung open the front door in my face and brought down the soot yet again.

This morning (Sunday) from Bridge School, Weald-stone, we sent almost fourteen hundred children away to Holyhead and Chester. (Bridge School was a collection-point.) This lot was more cheerful, perhaps due to their numbers. Was up to my neck in papers for Tuesday last's parties. Naturally, careful lists have to be compiled of the children – ages, addresses, nearest relatives, notes as to special care or medication in some cases – also of the teachers who go with them and see them settled in. Labels have to be written out and instructions stereo'd for the teachers. This morning Miss Bell from one of the Depart-ments upstairs found, as she said: 'Beardmore and his boss chasing each other round the table with sheafs of paper in their hands.' So the good soul dropped her own work to come and help, and by late morning we had three more volunteers doing the drudgery of listing and writing out labels. Sneaked off home and slept for one and a half hours so that I could get back and work this evening. When I left the place Registrations for evacuation were being phoned in continually.

7 *August, Monday*

Perfect weather for an August Bank Holiday, if we could have an August Bank Holiday.

This morning the Controller called me into his office and again mentioned that I should take over Information at incident-sites. But this time he enlarged on the kind of incident we might expect in the future, from rocket-bombs, of which he had been forewarned by Whitehall. He envis-aged forty-five acres of devastation, the formation of eight information centres on the periphery, and a central office for administration. He moved the lid of his tobacco-tin over a map of the Urban District to demonstrate that fixed information offices would be wiped out with everything else. Therefore some form of mobile office, as for instance trucks from the Surveyor's Department, would be required. And what happens to communication with the central office when phone-wires, perhaps the exchange itself, are put out of action? I suggested that the Home Guard were sited everywhere, as were the Street Marshals of Civil Defence, and while he h'mmed agreement the unspoken comment was that, for no good reason that I know of, hostility existed between the Home Guard and the Civil Defence. I was told to go away and think about it but obviously it's too big for me, although if it comes it will have to be faced. I am essentially a field-man, interested only in individuals.

In the afternoon I was planning with the departmental head for an adaptation of the old 'Mass Raiding Billeting' which entails forcible billeting of strangers on any given household, never a happy or successful remedy. He had dug the plan out of a bottom drawer and it was dated, interestingly enough, as early as 1937 and 1938. The plan was devised to meet the needs of up to 20,000 homeless, when it was imagined that the main arteries out of London would be packed with fleeing humanity, carts, cars, lorries, etc. Now I know why all these feeding-bottles, rubber teats, teaspoons, tins of dried milk, folding camp-beds and chairs, appear in the inventories of Rest Centres. An awful feeling that I shan't be able to face it if it comes.

The new baby is thriving and Jean is already walking. Victoria is at Finchley with Aunt Betty because I didn't have the time to see to her small needs. All three will go to Freda's in Yorkshire when Jean is strong enough. 'What I really want,' she says, 'is to find myself in my own big bed again', and I didn't have the heart to tell her, that, if she and the new baby stayed at home, they would have to sleep in the Surface Shelter.

This is a race against time, ourselves against the rockets which our armies (one hopes) are soon to put out of action.

13 August

A blazing brass sun. The daytime heat followed by the cold air pouring in through open windows at night (left open out of regard for blast – who doesn't remember the early days when we were adjured to shut doors and windows tight and paste the latter over with sticky-tape!) gives me a runny nose and a tight chest. The consequent Ephedrin is at this moment making my handwriting shaky.

Times are not so urgent. We are all of us suffering from the depression of anti-climax. I have quarrelled with Gates, who absented himself for a fortnight when we were beset with fly-bombs and had evacuation of children on our hands, and one of the Welfare ladies isn't speaking to the other. The old antagonism of permanent staff for us war-time recruits is never far away. When the next crisis comes I daresay we shall all be one happy family again. I propose going sick for two days as a temporary remedy.

Anthea was born with a slight discoloration of the right eyelid and a mark on the top lip, both of which, we are assured, will fade. Otherwise I am told that she is 'a lovely baby' and I must say she looks it to me, with or without the heat-spots covering her face and torso. I was prepared for her to be in some way imperfect because of the pace we live at, the duckings for cover, the unconscious fear that even Jean cannot remove. Her composure is beyond praise. I don't know how she does it. Her only anxiety was that confounded plate-glass door, not the birth itself. She is sure that the Old Redding bomb didn't shatter it only because it's loose on its runners and has a certain amount of give. Victoria rejoices to be back home again, and Jean hates the idea of having to leave her home, even though I have warned her of the danger of rocket-bombs.

Throughout my life August has been the bloody month, when people die and awful things happen. At this moment I guess that the crucial battle of the invasion of Europe is being fought somewhere between Caen and the Seine, where the Germans are said to be boxed in. But to look onto the quiet street, from which almost everyone has retreated because of the heat, and to hear the Band of the East Surreys striking up in Headstone Manor Park over the rooftops, who can possibly imagine tank-battles, fly-bombs, rockets, and the execution of prisoners.

19 August

A fly-bomb has just landed somewhere locally. I'll lay evens that the phone will go in twenty minutes or less. What happens immediately a bomb has fallen is that the ARP Incident Officer phones the Control Room which brings the services into action – the Surveyor's Heavy Rescue squad to dig out the dead and wounded, the hospital ambulance-service, the gas, water and electricity services. The Controller himself is contacted, wherever he may be, and he phones my boss, who phones me. I get on my bike with my little case and in forty minutes (no use my arriving sooner) I am on the spot.

The Controller has appointed me Information Officer for 794, which is the number of the Whitehall Circular relating to rockets. I had grotesque fears that the whole thing would fall on my shoulders but no, it's team-work again. The appointment has to be official both to give me status and to satisfy people like the Cashier who makes up wage-packets. Worth mentioning that for the week ending 12 August my gross wage was £14/3/4, less income-tax of £4/16/- and other deductions of 3/4d leaving a take-home pay of £9/4/-. So I didn't tell the truth to those would-be Heavy Rescue strikers.

The baby is prospering although she has an extra large pimple on her head which we don't know what to do with. She is pretty quiet even though fly-bombs shake the house and her first siren went off three hours after her birth. After the 6 p.m. feed she is put down in the sling-cot in the downstairs back room with Victoria, windows wide open and chicken-wire and curtains drawn. After the 10 p.m. feed she is transferred to the shelter of a chair within the chimney-breast recess. All the same, a neighbour with a new baby four doors away takes it into the Surface Shelter and if it cries, it cries.

First reports this morning of the Americans in Paris after their snaring and annihilation of that section of the German front facing them. Something to remember – at the movies last night, the expression on the face of the old lady of Chartres as she smashed a picture of Hitler to the ground.

27 *August*

Last Wednesday I took the family to Wharfedale, Yorkshire, to give them a holiday at my brother Alan's house, near Wetherby. I shan't easily forget waiting at 4 a.m. on the platform of Doncaster Station for a crowded train to come in, full of troops. Victoria sat on a suitcase and counted the number of stars she could see – interesting, really, because necessarily she had never seen stars before, except while on the run between the house and the Shelter. The baby howled her tiny head off, and who can blame her. They are safe for a time and Jean is rested, although the experience would seem to underline the maxim that one should never, in wartime at least, leave one's home. Yesterday I was swimming with a jolly party of people in the Wharfe and today I am at home again and not liking the loneliness, another Bomb Bachelor.

Up there they know nothing of fly-bombs and the threat of rockets. To them it was a story, something you hear before passing on to matters of real interest, like the Roses' match at Leeds. Only Freda kept on asking: 'But weren't you frightened, weren't you frightened?' leaving Jean and me to wonder whether we had been frightened or not. I suppose we had, but in moments of crisis one is too busy racing to pick up Victoria and find shelter for ourselves.

Since Wednesday Paris has been liberated, Bulgaria has asked for an armistice, and Roumania has been granted one. But let us get control of the fly-bomb and rocket sites before we rejoice. The Alert sounded as I was walking down the platform at St Pancras, and one of the abominable things passed dead overhead as I was waiting in Euston for the train to pull out.

11 September, Sunday

We seem to be emerging from a nightmare whose effects are still so much with us that we have to be convinced that we are awake. Since last Tuesday, 31 August, when at 10.30 p.m. a fly-bomb tore across the sky in a blaze of searchlights – not that they were needed because the bomb ejects a stubby tail of fire – we have seen no more of them. The Alert has not sounded for days. I have taken the beds upstairs and reconverted the back room into our parlour again from its temporary identity as a shelter. At the office we have nothing to do. Blackout regulations are being lifted. Evacuation has stopped. The Home Guard is no longer compulsory. No more daylight fire-watching. 'Do I wake or dream?'

Soon, I daresay, the old Siegfried line will be crossed and Germany invaded. The papers vie with each other in whipping up hatred against the Germans. At one time a hate-the-Germans campaign was being waged officially among the armed forces, but was frowned upon by the Church and then quietly dropped. I am not so fond of Germans myself but I don't promise what a friend of mine promises that he will never again shake hands with either a German or an Irishman – the latter because Ireland's farcical neutrality is forbidding us use of the western ports in the U-boat campaign. I go to retrieve my family on Thursday next and expect to bring them back on Tuesday week. Meanwhile I am painting here and there, I have boxed in the sink at last and fitted a new draining-board, painted the little go-cart red and yellow for when the baby shall need it, and I have trimmed the hedges – all because Jean is soon to come home.

The publishers tell me they sold two thousand copies of *The Staffordshire Assassins* before publication.

20 *September*

Yesterday I brought the family back, a long tedious journey on which both children were exemplary. They too seemed to want to get back to their home again almost as much as their mother. Fly-bombs have resumed. There was an hour's Alert last night in which we heard four familiar drones and 'Whoomps' but thank heavens in the distance. We have been entreated by the Government to leave mothers and children in the country but Jean loves her home too much to obey. And so, I suppose, do all the other mothers and children with whom we travelled. Prams and cycles choked the main termini – St Pancras and Euston – our coach was like a seaside excursion, and on the arrival platform were waiting fathers and husbands, lined up two or three deep.

No word yet from any source about the mysterious bangs we have been hearing, not preceded by the familiar droning in the sky. A crater appeared at Kingsbury in my absence, also a terrific mid-air explosion last Saturday which the old sweats at the office said 'shook the building'. The first of the explosions took place in the direction of Acton, followed by a rumour that it was a Home Guard arms-dump blowing up. Also a rumour that a plane had crashed with its bomb-load. Not until I had reached the last house in Stonegrove (I am on the hunt for billets for nurses again) did an old lady called Emery say: 'I'm afraid they've found something else.' The third theory, that we are being bombed from the stratosphere, has been replaced by the more probable one of rockets. If indeed they are caused by rocket-bombs, or should it be rocket-shells, then we can take heart because the devastation isn't a tenth of what was described by the lid of the Controller's tobacco-tin.

Terrible to think of the ferocity with which the RAF and American Air Force will attack Germany this coming winter. Horror stories begin to come in of execution-rooms and torture-chambers found in liberated cities, and of vast concentration-camps of starving disease-ridden Jews. After 2,000 years this would seem to be the final answer to Christianity as a practical mode of life, at least as practised between nations.

17 October

Journal temporarily held up by a fly-bomb which arrived on the 5th (Thursday) about 8.15 p.m. behind Methuen Road and Camrose Avenue, Edgware. Seventy-four houses rendered uninhabitable and the usual five fatalities. (The average in Harrow is five.) The WVS and I manned the office on site for four days and emerge with credit, particularly the WVS.

One of the notable incidents was our endeavour to trace the natural son of a man, who, with his wife, were numbered among the five. Apparently he had been a bad lot, for none of the legitimate issue and relatives generally would say much about him. His half-brother, a naval lieutenant, would not admit to the missing man's existence but maintained that he had no brother, which contradicted what the local postman had to say. This lieutenant, who had been given compassionate leave, arrived in uniform bringing his pretty wife with him. In reality, he was deeply ashamed of these, his humble origins, and hated having to bring his wife with him. You could almost hear him apologising as his wife preceded him, picking her way in her high-heeled shoes among the rubble. However, it was my business to find the half-brother, if he still existed. I traced his 1939 employers, ascertained that he was in the Corps of Military Police and that his wife lived in Uxbridge. Now I learn that he is separated from his wife while the CMP Records Office cannot identify him as one of theirs, presumably because he is using another name. But the search goes on. (Eventually he was traced, by the CMP, even though he was not and never had been one of their number, to the Green Howards and to a temporary residence at the Glasshouse at Aldershot. It's nice to be able to report that he was released for the funeral in the care of a CMP corporal and stood side by side with his naval half-brother at the graveside. Or so I was told by the WVS lady who also attended. She had been the only one present to appreciate the subtleties of the situation.)

I was worn out by the Tuesday and three days did not see me with my reservoirs of energy replenished. The constant adjustment of oneself to the understanding of the enquirer, coupled with irregular meals snatched at a mobile canteen, working in a shattered room, and throwing out confidence to counter distress, call for a robustness which I simply do not possess. So nervous energy supplies the deficit.

The phenomenon of 'bomb-happiness' was never more apparent. A man appeared first thing in the morning with blood-stains down the front of his shirt and joy all over his face. (When I say 'first thing' I mean three in the morning.) He couldn't stop talking. As well as I can remember, he said: 'I've lost everything. Suddenly – bang – just like that. I can't even find my wife! Nobody seems to know. Would you believe it. 1944. Ration-books, marriage-certificate, my father's letters to my mother, kid's birth-certificate – the whole lot. Well, I mean, what can you do! We were asleep. I've come to ask if you know where Christine is . . .' And so on, waving his arms and appealing to an audience of other victims in between laughs.

I was able to tell him that his wife and little girl were in hospital, neither of them seriously injured, and he went off just as he was, before we could stop him, to see them. He turned up again about 9 a.m., a wreck of a man, grey-faced, utterly and profoundly depressed, with twitching hands and restless feet, exhausted to the point of collapse, and partly deaf. I daresay the medics have gone into the question of why a man who had just lost all he has put together in a massive explosion should feel exalted and talkative: I put it down to an elementary relief at finding himself alive.

Last night I began to read C.R.W. Nevinson's *Paint and Prejudice* with its account of high jinks among pre-1914 students and celebrities. 'I have missed it all,' I thought, 'even though I've got more in me than half these lads.' Then I threw the book down because he seemed intolerably smug and bumptious and went upstairs to look at Victoria asleep. She's had gastric influenza and on Monday was like a hot sausage, tight, smooth, and hot to touch. I brushed the hair out of her eyes and thought that I hadn't done so badly, after all.

1 November

The Controller has recommended me for a job with the UNRRA *in Germany* at a rest camp or rest camps to be set up for Allied nationals who have been dispossessed, as also for the inhabitants of slave-labour camps as they are overrun. Allman, too, from Surveyor's. We are the only two to be so invited. It may be the job I was born for. But Jean? Would my health stand up to it?

We are sleeping downstairs again. The terrific double-bangs we hear come once or twice nightly and are now thought to be rocket-shells which are thrown up from somewhere in Norway (?Bergen), guided in their first twenty-five miles of ascent by beam, and allowed to descend 'roughly' over Great Britain. But because they are dropping just anywhere, in the North Sea, the Irish Sea, and the Atlantic, apart from in Colindale last night and Shenley (near Elstree) the night before – the Government is preserving a vast silence about them, as though they didn't exist. Also the German wireless gives no hint of their release. The situation is truly absurd, as though in the last war the Germans had released a salvo from howitzers and said: 'Let's keep absolutely mum about it and pretend it was never sent', and the Front Line generals had replied: 'All right then, we aren't going to admit that we've received the message.' Or an agreement to keep quiet about an earthquake, which is what these things are. They burrow thirty or more feet into the ground and there explode, throwing up a large crater, and destroy not by blast, like the fly-bombs, but by earth-tremor, so that a factory may seem intact from the outside and be in ruins within.

Theories run round the office about the reason for the quick double-bang, which incidentally seems more terrifying than the fly-bomb's drone-and-thump. One explanation is that the first bang is caused by the initial impact with the ground (or building) and the second bang by the thing's explosion. Or the Doppler effect may be responsible. Depending upon where you are in relation to the rocket – in front, immediately under, or behind – you hear a scream in mid-air before, during, or after the explosions. It often happens that you first hear the explosion and then the scream of its passage decreasing to a wail. Some wit has said that if you listen long enough you can hear the inventor's pencil on the drawing-board.

The blast appears to be more powerful than that of the fly. To Jean and me, our street gives the impression of being a thin unprotected ribbon with the playing-fields on one side and the willow-wood on the other, rendering us peculiarly defenceless against blast, flying glass, and tumbled chimney-pots. We have brought the single bed downstairs and Victoria is tucked into one end while Jean sleeps at the other. The baby sleeps in her carry-cot behind a chair within the recess of the chimney-breast in the dining-room (that is, we sleep in the back, the baby in the front). As for me, I occupy the divan next to Jean and Victoria.

15 *November*

Jean's thirty-fourth birthday. To cheer her up, I say that she has as long to live again plus two years. She is profoundly grateful that in the present emergency she isn't carrying the baby and can therefore nip about more easily – the baby is now on her own, so to speak. Something very profound about this.

No news yet of UNRRA. I am glad to have been picked out but don't think I want to go. Churchill has at last confirmed that we are under attack from rockets. A noisy night last night and three more bangs today. One that shook us at our lunch-table landed at Lewisham the other side of London, the best part of twenty miles away.

Apart from the unfortunates who cop it, most of us think that the bang is the most destructive part of the weapon. That's not true, of course. Jean says she doesn't fear the rockets so much as the fly-bombs. Something profound about this, too – rockets after all are only a development of the pistol, which we know about, but those pilotless robots carrying their load of destruction are uncanny. So far in Harrow we have escaped the rockets, so we don't know what destruction they cause. All we know is that in comparable districts they each kill five people, on the average, wreck a lot of homes, and frighten children. But how can they affect the outcome of the war? The answer is, not at all. They are senseless.

Much worry trying to find billets for the nurses at Stanmore Orthopaedic Hospital. I tell the boss that districts such as Stonegrove are exhausted and that the hospital must resign itself to lodging their nurses, say, at Elstree, and bringing them in by bus. But it won't do – the department has been given the job of finding billets more locally, and this we must do. Who can blame householders, already overtaxed, overworked, and overworried, for not taking them in, with the added burden of having to provide a room and board for a mere guinea a week! As one woman said before shutting the door on me: 'Just leave me alone and let me survive, if I can.'

A cold blue November. Blue not of the sky but of the bare branches, particularly in frost. Each year the vivid colouring of the leaves, especially of the horse-chestnut, is a new surprise. Yet the colouring is only a sympton of decay.

17 December

The grimmest Christmas to date but still, as Victoria grows older, it takes on more importance. The tree is set up with its gew-gaws, mostly home-made, and some presents have already been spread around it, arriving from nowhere as is the magic custom with presents. Ted and his daughter are coming to share Christmas dinner. Ted promises to cook it because the baby must have her usual meals, Christmas or no. He takes the place of the wretched German prisoner we had last Christmas, from the PoW camp at Hatch End – a bit of a failure, that, because I know no German and he had acquired little English. What he chiefly wanted was a water-proof pair of shoes. When I gave them to him he begged me by signs and words we knew like 'bitte' for a note to go with them saying that they had been freely given. He managed to tell us that when the Commandant had called four of them into his office to say that the invitation had been received (i.e. mine) they hadn't believed him. A Bavarian. Hadn't Sergeant Grischa been a Bavarian?

31 December

Eight days of fog and ice. Perhaps these are responsible for an oppression of the mind like a grey rain cloud, unpleasantly like the persistent one that kept me apathetic for five weeks at Bletchley.

While I think of them, two fatuosities I have committed this war: (1) buying in rice and condensed milk in October, 1939, and (2) gas-proofing the little bedroom. Of course, there are worse examples than these, I think because I was made to do them. If I had used my own common sense I would never have gas-proofed the little room – nor for that matter gone with the BBC to Droitwich. When this is all finished, I am going to be my own master and commit fatuosities for which I alone will be responsible.

I enjoyed Christmas Eve better than the Day itself, visiting people in the hard frost and brilliant sunshine with the two infants. Victoria is still piping: ' 'Way in the Manger'.

1945

28 January, Sunday

We are suffering, here at home, the worst period of the war. We are all – all of us, at the office, in the shops, and at home – weary of war and its effects. Intense cold has arrived (my feet at this moment are resting on a hot-water bottle and the panes are frosted over) with snow, ice, hail, and sudden clashes of thunder that go to make the illusion that we are on the Russian front. The V2 rockets also help the illusion. Four mornings in succession they have woken us up – not bangs so much as prodigious muffled explosions which resound in all quarters at once, reverberating for about ten seconds. The blast is upon us before we know it, blowing out curtains, rattling doors, and doing its usual trick of jolting up the loft trap-door. Well, trap-doors can be put back into place, so I don't grumble, or try not to. At 4 a.m. yesterday one landed on the fringe of a spinney on Stanmore Common. I inspected it in the line of duty, the usual crater as big as a room with felled trees pointing outwards from it, like a small-scale meteoric crater in Siberia. The nearest houses (well-to-do) had ceilings down and windows caved in and rows of fluttered tiles. 'Fluttered' means that for five seconds or more they are jerked up by blast with the result that when they fall back again they either shatter or are displaced. No casualties, thank heavens, and not much damage otherwise. The fright that it caused was out of all proportion.

Gas and electricity are cut off at times but so far not in Harrow. Potatoes are scarce. Coal and boiler-fuel also. By this I mean that we do a vast amount of scheming and worrying to obtain these things. I should not like to add up the number of fruitless expeditions I have made in the search for paraffin. On my rounds, when I see a queue of people with cans outside an ironmonger's, I make it my business to hurry home and fetch our cans and join 'em. Owing to these endeavours we have not so far run short of our creature comforts. But Mrs Amos next door looks pinched and half-starved.

The Russian winter offensive has brought their armies to within a hundred miles of Berlin. The German fronts are closing in – Upper Silesia, for example, is in Russian hands, while all East Prussia, hotbed of German militarism since Frederick the Great, and for all I know earlier, is only waiting for the *coup de grâce* before it capitulates. As I read of Germans working with pistols on their desks, of German refugees being ordered off the roads, of German evacuees riding back to safety on the buffers of railway-carriages, of German towns and villages being razed – I remember the machine-gunning of Canadian prisoners after Dieppe, our own Hampden Road bomb when the air was full of feathers from mattresses and housewives were screaming, the Lublin Castle tortures – yes, and Anthea wrapped in shawls because of the cold waking up to wail when the Stanmore rocket fell.

Snowflakes are falling although the sun has been trying to bore a hole through the snow-clouds. Jean is just hurrying outside to put the stove on in the Shelter before returning Anthea to her nest of shawls in the dining-room, while Victoria, her head full of the Primary School she has begun to attend, sits on the hearth-rug rattling her beads and marbles about on a tray and saying: 'Now, I want all Junior Mixed on this side, please.' And here I sit with a dressing-gown over my clothes writing about them.

19 February

I live in the enchanted world of illness when the mind is

freed from the everyday and travels through landscapes where all is light and people pass like sunbeams. Too much Ephedrin has given me some sleepless nights and Corky has laid me off for a week with the convenient label of nervous debility.

A fortnight ago I was sent on loan to Islington to help make up past work for their Rehousing Department. This was on the recommendation of the Area Supervisor of Rehousing, a term that includes seeing to the needs of the bombed-out. Islington has an enviable ARP Centre but I don't know that I was able to do much as it was a desk job that needed local knowledge. A fly-bomb there kills up to thirty people and has been known to put two hundred people into the Royal Free. However, on the same recommendation I was sent a week ago to Wood Green, north London. Here was the usual shattered Information Office and the now-familiar sounds of the clink-clink of tilers at work, roaring of lorry engines, and clittering of glass near the crater of a rocket that had landed on the Artisans & General Noel Park Estate, which had left eighteen dead and eighty houses in ruins.

The first of my two days there was made memorable by my actually seeing a rocket explode in mid-air. The weather had been cold and foggy and, mug of tea in hand, I was at the front door, admiring a patch of blue sky for its rarity. A puff of smoke appeared inside the patch and there slowly slid out of the smoke a white-hot speck followed by a sleeve of whitey-brown smoke. I had time to go inside, say to the fellows busy with their sheets of injured: 'Hey, d'yer want to see a rocket?' and return to the threshold before two great bangs sounded. The pieces are supposed to have fallen over Acton.

After the Wood Green experience I was tired out but couldn't sleep – had a rotten night wheezing on Saturday – and here I am.

Good thing that when I'm poorly Jean is fine, and vice versa, but even she is beginning to feel the pull of the season and six months' attention to the newest tyrant.

30 *March*

Another rocket, and worst of the lot, landed at the top of Uppingham Avenue. I remember some time ago cycling down Weston Drive into Uppingham and thinking that if a rocket landed there it would make a right mess. And it had, if only because the damned thing had landed plumb on all three mains – water, gas, electricity. Water and gas had become mixed with the result that far down the hill in Kenton householders were being warned by loud-hailers from police-vans not to make use of any of the services. I don't have anything to do with the service engineers but, my word, they had arrived first according to report, and were still busy repairing and making up when I left.

The rocket had landed at 3.40 in the morning, killing nine people among whom was a 9-year-old boy who had been flung out of bed, through the rafters, and into a back garden ten houses away – at first, nobody had been able to find him.

As I watched the mass funeral (Union Jack, Bishop of Willesden, Civil Defence, WVS, and the Controllers' cars lined up for three hundred yards) tears came to my eyes not with the grief and distress caused to survivors but with the incalculable trouble to which they will be put, months and years of it, before they can resume any sort of normal life and the incident becomes only a tale to tell to the grand-children. Even obtaining an everyday thing like soap has its problems, let alone the replacement of identity-cards, ration-books, personal papers, with which I can give some help. In fact, I suggested to the WVS that they leave some bars of soap in my office for dispensation; it duly arrived, and within a day it had all gone. Also here for the first time

I had an official from Public Assistance sitting at my side, giving away money – not loaning, giving.

This incident was also made memorable by the office I had set up suddenly catching fire, provisionally put down to a short in the electricity supply creating a spark that set alight a small gas-leak. Luckily only seven or eight of us were inside the house, and we managed to get out in a mad scramble without casualty. A moment later, in the street and watching the blaze, which had started at the back, I remembered the infinite pains with which the WVS had gathered and collated information about the inhabitants of the affected houses before and after. Without thinking twice about it I threw myself inside, swept the papers up in my left arm and while shielding my face with my right arm bolted outside again. The only damage resulted from the right side of my head catching fire. At least, there was a strong smell of burning and I found the hair singed off. No medals for rescuing papers. Now if they had been a baby instead . . .

After three days at the Information Centre I was limp as a wet rag and have not yet fully recovered.

Another reason why I am limp is the row going on downstairs. With the plum-blossom hanging over newly watered loam and pear-blossom shaking against the various cloudscapes, I would ordinarily be thinking of spring and digging but downstairs workmen are replacing the ceilings. This ceiling campaign began last Wednesday when, having brought down the ceilings in our bedroom, they replaced the plaster with thistle-board. Yesterday they did the same for the children's room. And tomorrow it is the turn of the bathroom and the dining-room. Apparently the rockets have widened the cracks created by the fly-bombs landing in Bellfield Avenue, Headstone Drive, and Cumberland Avenue. We live hand-to-mouth in an atmosphere of dust, billeted in our own back room. These three, sometimes

four, workmen have visited each house in the avenue in
turn, starting at the Headstone Lane end. Every house
down there has either got a pile of broken plaster and dust
outside its front door or the householder, if a gardener with
an eye for some free lime, has spread it over his vegetable
patch. The technique for replacing a ceiling is to mount a
low sturdy table or stool and hit the plaster with a sledge-
hammer. Down it all comes in slabs and pieces which then
have to be cleared up. In come the large rectangles of
thistleboard which are sawn into shape *in situ* and then
positioned aloft and nailed onto the upstairs rafters. Close
the doors and seal it as we may, the dust always manages to
find its way into our hair and tea and the food in the pantry.
The whole job is being carried out under contract to the
Surveyor's Department and is free of charge.

Last week the famous crossing of the Rhine at Remagen.
According to the press one might think that we had had
little opposition (Frankfurt taken, General Patton eighty-
five miles into Westphalia) but my guess is that such optim-
ism is on a par with the paucity of news about rockets. Here
at Harrow we hear some of the bangs and occasionally get
the things ourselves but according to Jean's aunt at Black-
heath (not wholly reliable, I shouldn't think) they hear and
sometimes get four every hour. Group reports come
through daily as 48 dead or 119 dead or 22 dead. Only as far
away as Buckinghamshire the peasantry knows nothing of
rockets, and in Manchester all they learn is from one line of
news in the paper: 'In south England there was some enemy
activity. Casualties and damage are reported.' As I said
before, it's like trying to conceal news of an earthquake.

I can't close this Easter report without remarking the
always astonishing revival of things, feathery willow-tops
looking extremely Covent Garden, daffodils holding little
pools of rainwater, apple-blossom pink just showing as the
petals unfold, grass a yellow viridian, and little 'triljen'

(Victoria's word) out with their skipping-ropes on the pavement.

K. is for corner, K. is for cup,
This is the day we all break up.

26 April

I have the billeting of nurses on the brain. Canvassing for voluntary billets, always a degrading business, has produced nothing so now I am faced with compulsory billeting, which is worse. Oddly enough, the foreign refugees, some of them Jewish, are the least receptive, not to say hostile. This morning there came a frantic call from the Hospital almoner to say that one of the girls had had two Alsatians patrolling outside her room all night so that she wasn't able to reach the bathroom. I daresay the family owning the Alsatians, whom the Department had rehoused in 1940, felt that they had suffered enough interference from authority.

Took a Luminal last night but the eyes are still tired. The ceilings are now distributed over the garden and I have made several sowings, but apart from main crops like runner-beans, tomatoes, and brussels, I shan't spend much energy there.

In the foregoing there is no hint that this morning's paper told us that the Russians had now completely encircled Berlin and occupied one third of it, nor that the full horror of the Concentration Camps at Belsen and Buchenwald was the chief topic in press and radio. Only confirms my general finding that people are impossible but individuals unique and precious. Rockets came to a halt about a month ago, on Monday we were given permission to leave our blackouts undrawn, and enamel saucepans have returned to the shops. The late evenings are quite wonderful, so quiet, with the lights from windows slanting across the street and shining on the almond-trees' new foliage, and neighbours coming out in the mild air to gossip over their front gates and fences.

I am laying in all the coal I can find, at whatever price, because although the war may be in its closing stages we have yet to pay for it.

6 May, Sunday

Eyes still very tired, which makes me irritable because I have a clear weekend and don't feel like doing anything. This last weekend has at last brought us the surrender. The office and for all I know all the world are now waiting for the signal officially to take two days' holiday. Two days after five years of it seems a trifle inadequate. But we cannot officially celebrate until the Russians have broken up the last resistance in Austria and Czechoslovakia. Meanwhile our thirst for prodigies is exhausted – the Bad Man and Goebbels dead, Berlin taken, fighting finished throughout north Germany, the final surrender – all within seven days.

21 May, Whit Monday

I remember that in the past – how long ago! – Coronation Day was ruined for me by lack of sleep. Now our two Victory Days were almost ruined by bronchitis, very fittingly if one bears in mind the attacks I had during the war, but all the same I made myself join in the bonfires, the staying-up when I wanted to be in bed, and the fireworks. Jean made a really lovely supper to which the Kieffers came, *père et mère* for Bob is still in Alex., Ted and his handsome daughter (one hour ten minutes late but we had started without her) and for which Victoria was allowed to stay up. The curtains were left undrawn because a community spirit is abroad and everyone wants to share in every one else's rejoicings. All the searchlights shone in the sky, the office-girls and Gates went up to Town to join the vast

crowds in front of Buckingham Palace, and the whole business was clouded by impending trouble with Russia over
the future of Poland.

I must be anti-social because I find that rejoicing with a
hundred thousand others isn't my idea of fun, or even of
celebration. We have come to the end of it all with only the
loss of Jean's mother. Our home is intact, our children have
been safely born and raised without (so far as we can see)
impairment, and our purpose in this, our unique life, has
not been lessened. On the contrary, it has been advanced.

3 June, Sunday

Food is scarce. Most days I go to the British Restaurant for
a mid-day meal. I suffer from stretches of lassitude, mostly
in the evening when I usually like to go gardening. I put it
down to deficiencies in this or that protein or vitamin. But
there's no lack of energy in the baby. Before 6.30 this
morning she had put an arm through her cot and lifted the lid
off a box of Baby Powder which she partly ate and mostly
spread round the room, making Jean sneeze and wake up.

Now the added and inevitable reason for not taking in a
nurse as lodger: 'But the war's over, isn't it?' Trouble is, I
see the householders' point of view much too clearly.

10 June

Cecil Madden tells me that *The Staffordshire Assassins* is on
sale on every bookstall from here to Plymouth, plus an extra
big display at Peter Jones' in Sloane Square. I know that it
must be moving because, when pushing my bike up the
back road to Harrow-on-the-Hill, I noticed a copy in a small
shop that usually sold only comics, tobacco and cough-
drops. Nevertheless, characteristic of my career, the publishers are reluctant to take *Madame Merlin* because it's a
war-book. And so we go on, lifted up by one wave only to
fall back into the trough of the next.

2 July, Monday

Election Day is 5 July. I have attended Mr Hugh Lawson's Common Wealth meeting, and one by Sir Hubert Young. I have no need to go to Norman Bower's Conservative Party meeting, and I shall hear Joan Thompson (Labour) tomorrow. None of them moves me very much because I haven't got the kind of mind that understands how a *country* can be governed. Last week we had a committee-meeting to discuss the subject of billeting nurses, about fourteen of us including my friend the Area Superviser, Gardner, and the Hospital Staff Secretary: no firm conclusion was arrived at and the chairman (Gardner) couldn't even govern the few of us round the table. In fact, I am so naive politically that my mind goes fondly back to the era of the Benevolent Despots, men who wanted to rule, enjoyed ruling, and ruled well, according to their respective fashions. My favourite character in history 'is practically unknown, Hieron II of Syracuse, who ruled his small dominion for over fifty years without ever having recourse to war, despite having the all-powerful, bloody-minded Carthaginians to the south and the up-and-coming Romans to the north. For Syracuse read 'Britain', for Carthage read 'Russia', and for Rome read 'USA'.

After all that I shall vote Liberal while Jean, having heard a broadcast by her favourite man, Beveridge, has come to the same decision.

Tuesday and Wednesday last forty of us assembled in the Wealdstone Council Chamber to dispatch Services Voting papers. We were busy from 7 a.m. to 9 p.m., under constant (friendly) supervision by the Clerk. On Thursday the 5th I am to serve as Polling Clerk somewhere.

4 July

Overheard two workmen talking in the Harrow Weald teashop, a favourite rendezvous for the Council workers.

Plumbers or gasfitters, I'd guess. 'Don't want him again.' A long look at the other man – so much is conveyed by looks and glances! He replied: 'Enough battles for one lifetime.' After a long pause and a sip of tea, the first man said: 'Bloody Russia', and this time looked down at the table, interested in a drop of tea that had fallen on his donkey-jacket. The second man said: 'The old cock's just aching to wave us up and at 'em again', to which the first man replied, having waited to see if the other was of the same mind: 'Catch me.'

They had been talking about Churchill and had thus agreed not to vote for him. Now multiply their little chat by tens of thousands and one gets the result of the Election. Those men weren't *for* Attlee, they were *against* Churchill who in other circles is known as the Happy Warrior.

7 *July*

By chance, or was it, I was given Victoria's classroom for my Polling Station. I walked down the street at 6.30 a.m. in an odour of limes after rain and returned home at 9.30 p.m. in sultry heat, having spent the whole day in the one hut. An 82% poll, quite extraordinary.

4 *August*

August Bank Holiday Saturday, and a glorious day at that, hot and still, the kind that knocks me down with a sledge-hammer and only lets me pick myself up again about 9 p.m. Elsewhere boats must be on the river, Margate sands must be filled with deck-chairs, and people are flocking together wherever people can flock together. Our small family will watch the cricket-match in Headstone Park this afternoon and if the crowds grow too thick we shall come back to our home and garden.

As for me, this morning I sit in the Wealdstone Council Office and write this as I wait for customers in search of

Council help to get somewhere to live. They see big houses lying empty at the end of overgrown drives and want to know why the Council isn't 'doing something'. The answer is quite simple, that the Council has no money available to renovate the big empty houses. Mills took me over one such in Marsh Lane that had lately been vacated by the WRNS. We found the roof leaking, fireplaces vandalised, kitchen sink in the middle of the floor, scabrous graffiti written on the walls of loos and bathrooms, and unmentionable objects peculiar to females stuffed behind the bath. No public body can allow access to such a hotch-potch. So, impasse, and because a Labour Government was returned so decidedly, here I sit, if only to show willing.

22 August

The silence between 4 August and now includes the dropping of the world's first and second Atomic Bombs on Japan and victory world-wide, with qualifications. I was never good at grasping or commenting on world-shattering events like this. My mind isn't big enough. My father used to say that he found himself having more sympathy with the cat next door breaking a leg than with thousands dying of floods in China or famine in India. It's much the same with me. I can't begin to imagine three square miles pulverised and so many thousand Japanese scorched to cinders. My instinct is to ask: 'Who's the Incident Officer?' and I remember the Controller's tobacco-tin lid travelling over the map of Harrow and my own feeble effort to cope with the situation – not even that, but with the possibility of such a situation.

7 October

Today, one of the best days of a rich summer, leaves are at their most colourful under a long yellow sun, with mists about, and the faint nostalgic sweetness of autumn – log-cutting, buttered crumpets, and fairy-tales all implied by a moment of silence in a wood otherwise filled with the rustling of falling leaves.

Now then, in the last analysis, which gives me more satisfaction, the foregoing, or a Victory celebration in Headstone Park with Home Guard explosives and Fire Guard incendiaries for fireworks? Why, across the park where one of the first fly-bombs had landed, new tiles are still visible on many of the houses, while I know, because it was my job, that many of the inhabitants were either killed or have left to try to begin new lives elsewhere. Who is to speak for the elderly Browns killed by the rocket that landed behind the Embassy Cinema and of which I pocketed a gyroscope by way of souvenir? Filled with similar thoughts, I guess, Jean said: 'Let's leave 'em to it and go home', and she turned the push-chair round while I caught Victoria's hand to bring her away.

14 December

Returned home through cold wet streets from checking the contents of the Rest Centre at Honeypot Lane to find Jean in tears. She held out a Curtis Brown envelope she had opened, the post having arrived late because of Christmas, and inside I found a cheque for £877/15/10, royalties on the sale of the 'Assassins'. I almost burst into tears myself. Only someone who knows the sheer quantity of writing I have done since I was seventeen – just twenty years ago – the early success of the Potteries novel followed by the long 1931 to 1938 gap in which I could get nothing published, the Walter Hutchinson humiliations, can appreciate our feelings. 'Our' because Jean was part of it, labour of typing, bitterness, and hope.

1946

---

3 March

Two wretched families have moved into one of our requisitioned mansions in Marsh Lane and are shortly to receive
an injunction to leave. Have twice visited them officially
and once unofficially, under pledge of secrecy, to give them
some clothes and blankets Jean has found for them. A scene
of squalor and misery rare even in these days. A bus
conductor, two women, and three schoolchildren, driven
desperate for somewhere to live, camp out in a large
dilapidated room without light, water and (yesterday at least)
without fuel for a fire. Sullen and dirty faces swollen with
colds, an orange-box scraped dry of all but coke-dust, two
saucepans on an unmade bed, a spirit-stove on which bacon
was frying, and a green teapot shaped like a racing-car on a
strip of newspaper many times ringed. I try to relate this
scene to the house's history of comfort and elegance,
perhaps a carriage or car at the front door, discreet servants.

1 April

This morning two typical rehousing cases. The first a
woman who had been abandoned at eighteen months and
was so ill-treated subsequently in an Institution that at 50
she had to carry a chair round with her, to sit on when she
felt faint – heart, and some spinal trouble. She was a
sub-tenant and technically a trespasser, and would be
turned out this week. Secondly, a woman of 28 with a child
of 5, in process of being divorced. She was living with her
husband's parents, and the husband was 'coming out' (of
Wormwood Scrubs) at the end of July.

We get dozens of such stories each week, some of them

more true than others. One has to make oneself approach-able and sympathetic but at the same time hold one's own self back. The customers play every trick to bring me over onto their side, and I must say that in their place I should do the same. After this experience I shall never again criti-cise a public authority without first hearing their side of the problem. They have factors to cope with that cannot be advertised.

Counter packed with customers, mostly women, wanting help in finding homes. They never fail to rouse interest. Behind their stock clichés, e.g. 'It's all very well for you behind your counter', and 'I pay my rates, always have', and 'You want to come and see for yourself', and the anger they pretend, is a dumb resignation and non-comprehension. Also experience has shown us what liars they can be. But behind all the words and counter-thumping lies some unknown factor sitting in judgment within them so that I have known a woman turn away in mid-argument and leave the office, not necessarily in anger, disgust, or despair, but because this other-self of hers has made the decision.

Have found this unknown arbiter in myself. Do or say what I will, this X-factor secretly passes judgment. Not conscience but, I suppose, a build-up of experience that has passed into the unconscious. It's impossible to convey in a novel although somewhere I referred to 'the strong-box of his commonsense'. Prince Andrew in *War and Peace* comes nearest to a portrayal of it. Coupled with the inadequacy of words and speech this ultimate X-factor makes nonsense of novels as a serious medium for describing human nature.

One house in particular, No 7, Elmshurst, large Victo-rian red brick hidden by overgrown laurel and privet, rouses greed and animosity. 'Mister, it's empty, the blinds have been drawn all winter. No milk-bottles, nothing. Why doesn't the Council take it and make flats of it?' I can't tell

them that somewhere inside lives an old man and two cats
who have made tracks through its dust and rubbish like the
tracks in a jungle. How people choose to live is no concern
of ours, and we are not allowed to requisition inhabited
property.

10 May

A familiar face at the counter this week, that of Fletcher,
my one-time superior at the BBC, Droitwich. Transpired
that before the war he had rented his house in Surbiton,
or subsequently sold it, I forget which. Either way, his
Department had returned to London and he was now
homeless. I gave him the familiar (and true) *spiel* that the
bombed-out were our priority and that anyway he was
Surbiton's concern. Then I took him home to lunch, having
first warned Jean.

When we arrived, there she was tricked out in her almost-
best (as I knew but Fletcher didn't) with the little ones
polished up likewise, walking out to greet us from the home
off which I had recently paid the mortgage. A nice easy
friendly lunch in the front room, in which we had sometimes slept during the air-raids and attacks by fly-bombs
and rockets. Only when he had left on his bike to pursue his
house-hunting did Jean say: 'If that isn't the sweetest
revenge.'

She was remembering when she had strolled down a
country lane to invite Mrs Fletcher to go for a walk with her
– and been snubbed. Jean had no doubt it was because I
had been a grade or two lower than her husband. I for my
part remembered that it was Fletcher, the supreme politi-
cian, who had blocked my transfer to a more congenial
department.

9 June

Rain began to fall at 11 a.m. yesterday and continued hard

and steadily until 11 p.m., much dampening the Victory celebrations. Early on I was digging over the ground for the runner-beans when Jean called me to the kitchen window to hear the broadcast of the parade which had reached the Mall. I arrived in time to listen to the announcer declare the arrival of the ten-ton bomb, 'largest missile ever conceived by man', and the cheers of the onlookers, which were enough to send me back to my digging.

Good God, have we forgotten already, or did we never learn?

Epilogue

George Beardmore was true to his word and gave up his job with Harrow Council to earn his living by his pen. However, it was as a writer for older children that he had most success, post-war. From 1950 to 1960 he worked on the remarkable children's magazines *Eagle* and *Girl* with Marcus Morris and Chad Varah, writing scripts for cartoon serials like 'Jack o' Lantern' and 'Belle of the Ballet'. He used the same characters in proper children's books.

'Those last few years after my fifty-eighth birthday until the retirement pension began with my sixty-fifth, I wonder how we survived . . . Three times, if I remember correctly, the Royal Literary Fund made a handsome donation, or we should have been sunk.' In 1967 he wrote the first of a series of five stories for teenagers set in the Hebrides. Jean died in 1973 and George survived her until 1979.

Appendix

Novels by the Author referred to in the text

Dodd the Potter, by Cedric Beardmore, Cassell & Co, 1931
The House in Spitalfields, by George Wolfenden, Hurst & Blackett, 1937
The Undefeated, by George Wolfenden, Hurst & Blackett, 1940
The Spy Who Died in Bed, by George Wolfenden, Hurst & Blackett, 1941
The Little Doves of Destruction, by George Wolfenden, Hurst & Blackett, 1942
All Space My Playground, by Cedric Stokes, Macdonald & Co, 1943
The Staffordshire Assassins, by Cedric Stokes, Macdonald & Co, 1944
Madame Merlin, by George Beardmore, Macdonald & Co, 1946